THANK YOU

I want to say thank you to Lauren Dunkin for sharing her time and unique talents by creating the book art and cover. Her expressive ideas and vision on life have been inspiring to me as I've watched her grow in her career. I admire how she sees simple concepts of any nature, and turns them into a framework of color and beauty. This motivation helps me see the world through a lens of originality and peace.

I want to thank my editor, Matthew Girard, for helping my dreams of writing come to fruition. His talents for seeing beyond the content and understanding the collective perspective are one of a kind. I'm not sure what the traditional role for editors looks like, but he went above and beyond the titles of a power hungry writer with a giant red pen! His words of encouragement, and ability to see past what most saw as "crazy," have allowed me to express my passions for helping people discover the best versions of themselves. His literary talents made this book possible and complete.

Lastly, I must thank the most important person of all - You. You the reader, you the amazing individual who is taking this journey with me, you the explorer of being healthy in all aspects. Without you, I never would have found my holistic identity or my Healthy ME. So thank you so much, because you are who give me purpose and meaning in life to continue being the best ME I can offer.

INDEX

INTRODUCTION TO HEALTHY ME, HEALTHY US

PART I: HEALTHY ME

Chapter 1: Healthy ME Defined
Chapter 2: Career and Purpose
Chapter 3: Self Exploration
Chapter 4: Fear
Chapter 5: Self Care and Identifying Stress
Chapter 6: Summary of Healthy ME

PART II: HEALTHY US
Chapter 7: Healthy US Defined
Chapter 8: Communication
Chapter 9: Sex and Sexual Communication
Chapter 10: Affection and Intimacy
Chapter 11: Financial Communication
Chapter 12: Conflict and Resolution
Chapter 13: Parenting
Chapter 14: Overcoming Betrayal
Chapter 15: Summary of Healthy ME Healthy US

INTRODUCTION

HEALTHY ME, HEALTHY US

It was all I could do to keep my mind spinning out of control, and my soul from being put to rest. One thought spiraling into negative oblivion. The crumb on the dish sitting there so delicately on the plate, starring, judging, taunting, and telling me, "I am the power that resides over you." And it was. Truth be told, it had full control over my future, my movements, my being — it dominated me.

As I hear the thoughts of people who come into my life on an every day chance, these are the prologues to the stories that they tell. A dish crumb that controls their next move, and voice that commands their focus, an aged wound that determines their future outcome. These are the stories they seek closure from, meaning to, and an escape to something better. These stories are told by you, by me, by your neighbor, your teacher, your mentor, your inner child, and your deep self within.

I started my path by seeing what not to follow; control of a partner, helplessness of daily instruction, self destructive coping, and loneliness. At one point, I understood escape to be the very culprit of this downward spiral, that being, finding identity from the opinions, ideas, accomplishments, and wisdom of others

1

who knew no worse, but no better than myself. I wanted the world to pick me because I understood fear as my forefront and my answer.

As I followed my own journey as a speaker, thinker, artist, and therapist, I saw the hidden meaning in all the prologues that darkened the thoughts of most people. I saw the hurt, pain, betrayal, and self doubt that lead most to believe they were in a sanctioned place of arrest. Most insightfully, I also saw the alternative paths. Paths that lead to greatness not silence, connections not solitude, accomplishment not failure, and most importantly, life versus forced death. I saw answers, resolutions, depth of human nature, hope, love, and a better humanity. I saw the true self, complexities, goodness, and all that hope and futures are built on. I saw you and what you hope to become.

The idea of the holistic self is built on facets that many of us miss. We are all built from hurt, joy, experience, cultural influence, sustainable focus, and expectations. Daily our roles change and find evolution from career, parenting, partnering, delivering, obligations, and individualism.

The roles in finding the best of us are also comprised of having a thorough understanding of what makes up who we are. Loving us for who we are, owning it, quirks and all. This is where healthy relationships stem from. This is where our journey begins and continues. This is where a healthy us is built.

This is a book for finding love, reconnecting, redirecting, love found and lost, single, gay straight androgynous. If you've ever second guessed yourself as a person and the relationships in your life, this book is for you.

PART I: HEALTHY ME

Chapter 1: HEALTHY ME DEFINED

I love and yet abhor intake sessions. The intake session is the first initial visit from a client. As a business-savy therapist, I have a few key points and goals in mind. Listen, identify patterns, create a treatment plan, articulate goals, build rapport, empathize, and then sell it. It being me, because as a therapist, I am the product. Oh, and by the way, I am conducting all of this thought process conjointly as I am also maintaining a composure "poker face," and looking like I am hanging out effortlessly and very matter of factly.

The love of intake is the beauty of vulnerability and raw articulation of the story presented by the client. It's full of passion, anger, confusion, and best of all, honesty. It has the ability to evolve, grow, edit, and takes on a life of its own. Why? Because it's genuinely human and true to form. This story has grown and formed a life of its own drenched in pain, sorrow, resentment, gratitude, lies, disdain, and has finally reached its form of simple truth. It is the bane of existence to the idea of being, well, stuck!

I abhor intake due to that exact reason. It's raw, it's beautiful, and it's truth; it's truth that no soul should ever bear, and yet it is what you, I, and all who breathe will at one moment or another will comprise and chalk up to as life. And for this very reason, I seek a better truth. I seek to facilitate a better meaning, a better purpose, and better outcome, and yes, hope.

Now, I'm no stranger to sarcasm or curse words, or by any means, the very raw stories my clients present. This is when I can relate, and I can create. I create hope, meaning, purpose, perspective, and options. This is where the birth of the healthy me begins. One person's unique story becomes the prelude to one person's unique conquest to an amazing adventure.

We are created with complexities that help us identify survival, danger, safety, gratification to basic needs, and stability. Yet, they are complex. All of these words have a different meaning to every individual. Our egos, traumas, and lives perpetuate into how we create what to make of all this. Our healthy selves are not formed by what we are given, but yet how we interpret what has, is, and will happen to us.

When we consider our whole selves, there are basic components to always keep in the forefront: Hobbies, partnerships, support systems, finance, family of origin, responsibilities, gaining positive attention, expectations, accepting and offering of love, and accomplishments. We hope to God our partners can just explain away half of this, and that the other half is just how we are built based on what we consider as "normal," but if that were the case, well we could just end this now, grab a drink, and continue on as we always have. But where does the fun in that fit in?

With each section of identifying the whole self, break down each segment into something manageable. What are my favorite hobbies? What brings me pleasure and joy? I don't care if I have someone to share it with; I don't need validation or approval. I just love it just for me, untainted, unwarranted of outside opinions, simply just love it for me. We struggle though with allowing such undefined content to happen due to clouded thoughts of time, productivity, pleasing others, and better yet, not being able to share it with someone.

A funny story I often share with clients is that of "reality" versus the infamous "social media reality,"
The story goes something like this.
A post on a social media site shows a beautiful picture of a dewy night, dark skies, slightly cloudy, with a bright view of light from a full moon. The caption reads, "Such a beautiful night for a walk outside." The picture and caption receive 88 "likes," thus achieving the approval of many soul searchers who wish they too could be out on this magical night. They go as far to daydream of what that moon may look like if they could be hand-in-hand with the person who posted this. They curiously

wonder what romance may lie in the bounds of that night, what the warmth of the hand who created this caption may feel like, how the love could evolve. This caption describing this picture is the essence of beauty, nature, romance, and hope from those in the oblivious abstract world of social media.

In truth, this picture was taken by a person who is in a deep conflict with his partner. After a non-resolved argument, he was asked to leave the apartment of his lover, where he stood with no vehicle, arms full with a hamper of clothes in one arm, half empty bottle of cheap vodka, and a 15-mile walk to the nearest place of residence. He had a phone with a camera, an ego that refused to be crushed, and a glimpse of hope that once this post was created, someone who saw the "social media reality" would soon comment, invite him in, and fulfill their "realty" of what fantasy could take place had they been under that moonlit picture of romance.

The point here is this: Your fantasy is based on your reality and your own will to see it through, even if your own truth is slightly skewed. How so? Your perspective of self is where the power resides. As people, we so often try to live vicariously through the better lives (or better perceptions we conceive) of others. We all do this at one point or another when we feel unfulfilled, small, and full of doubt. But knowing our own interests, passions, desires, and strengths gives us far more real promise

than that of dreaming to have the life of another.

Chapter 2: CAREER & PURPOSE

Blaring music screaming from my phone. A thoughtfully annoying setting I have applied to my phone to awake me from peaceful slumber telling me that now is the minute I must wake up. It doesn't compare to the light pink rainbow embroidered alarm clock I had as a 6-year-old. That alarm clock had hands. Three knobs allowed be to manually programed. One controlled the hour, another controlled the minute, and a third allowed me to move a tiny red stick that, by my best judgment as a first grader, would awake me with a soft buzz. Early enough to wake up and be at the bus stop before dawn. But now. Now, I have a finger-swiping digital machine that has placement for countless alarms, snoozes, and completely obstructive noises that I consider music during waking hours to tell me it is time to wake up, smile, and show up to work each with to fulfill my purpose.

As you can see, I am not appreciative of early mornings. I truly dislike being awake before the sun is out. I dislike crawling out of my warm cocoon of down-filled covers, and better yet, I despise being disrupted of my peaceful dreams full of cotton candy, sandy beaches, and undeniable joy. But I do this, each and everyday. And I recover, because I know after I mull over the trauma of disruption, I will quietly apply my makeup, pick out my clothing of expression for the day, and proceed to fulfill my duty, meaning, purpose, hell on some days, my obligation to existing on this earth. And once I'm in my office, my role as a therapist becomes alive and I take in the pleasure of serving those who may benefit from my existence. Yes, folks, this, by my terms, is the idea of meaning and purpose.

All to often I'll have clients come in searching for more. They want more money, more time, more appreciation, more recognition, more respect, and yeah, more power. They and myself always want more but typically, the more is not about the above described. It is far more beyond more! They want to know that they are contributing to the greater good.

I work with people from all walks of life, education, and career choice. Some are self-made entrepreneurs, some are in the service industry, and some are in transition from full-time homemakers seeking a new transformation based on curiosity and life opportunities (or mishaps that create opportunities). When I help these people explore who they really are and what they can truly contribute, I ask them one thing. "What can you do everyday that will make you feel like you served your purpose?" The title, paycheck, and time spent creating this piece of identity is so priceless and invaluable and yet, it is so overlooked when people are working through the pain that they harbor. I so firmly live by one quote: "Do a job you love, and you will never work a day in your life," by Confucius. This ideology is profound, simple, and justified.

For example, I typically explain career and purpose in this way: Those who chase a paycheck chase failure. When someone says, "I just need to make $50,000 dollars a year and I will be happy," I say, "well how do you intend to do that this month?" The year will break down in to months, weeks, and days. Each day is an op- portunity to contribute self worth, and without a plan, how do you intend to do so? But what if we changed the perspective from needing to make the figure of $50,000 dollars, to "I need to accomplish three things this month that will engage the people I want to contribute too." Personally, my example may look something like this. "This week I will book 20 clients, one out of three speaking events for the month, and one volunteer project." From this, I will charge for each event, fill my heart with personal achievement, and follow my intrinsic motivation to succeed in greatness. From this purpose-driven perspective, I am not focusing on a dollar amount to define or predict my worth and success. My purpose and organization of how I use my skills by the week will provide some instant gratification of accomplishment and mental comfort in achievements. Also, I charge fees for my services and distribution of skills; I am not blind to needing money to support myself and my children (keep in mind,

I have girls and they take after my love for adventure). The dollar amount is a result of me choosing clients and speaking events that are a good fit for me, leading to excellent customer service and a quality product, and ultimately building a reputable practice workshop series.

If I take the money-driven perspective, I would focus on saying "yes," to any kind of business that fell in my lap. This would lead to burnout, less time for continuing education, and a lack of self care. I may make a great amount of money temporarily, but long term, the money would be spent and my reputation would falter.

The fact is, following through with a good fit will systemically have a ripple effect on your personal, professional, and spiritual well being. This component of the holistic self will thrive all on its own and deeply impact the personal matters that contribute to you being a healthy component to a partnership. So many of my clients will become interested in this concept and then question it. They'll ask how their personality test makes a difference, what about education will help them, and where does the energy to keep going come from? My answers to these questions always go back to the basics; you have a family of influence, and you have the power to choose where you would like your voice to be heard.

Sometimes our fields chooses us, sometimes it is chosen for us, and sometimes, we evolve in to so much more than we could have ever imagined. Evolution happens everyday; exploring it and embracing it is what we do to really make it count. I reflect on my own career often. Stepping back and taking a look in, I think to myself, "who in their right mind would spend their time on earth listening to people's pains, heartaches, conflicts, despairs, and delinquencies? How can one person possibly sit for hours on end each and everyday absorbing the obscenities that we as humans endure daily and maintain an attitude of optimism and alternate positivities? How can one person make a living giving their whole selves to people who never emotionally, mentally, or physically ever give back?" And yet, I take responsibility for embracing what my intellect understood, and what the universe somehow picked me to do.

Career choice has a different significance to all of us. The idea is to base this relationship on trust and respect to our own level of intellect, beliefs, experiences, and most of all, passion! Finding our true career also establishes a healthy foundation for positive self identify and self worth so that we may establish purpose, integrity, and move forward to express our true desires. That of love, trust, and respect within our romantic partnerships.

Careers are not just built on paychecks. Seek

out your strengths and talents too. Often in my intake sessions, I describe my therapeutic style to clients and this usually includes my beliefs in positive psychology. The basic premise is that we have natural strengths but in the midst of feeling stuck, we tend to overlook what behaviors or habits we do daily that actually are working for us. These strengths are what we naturally can use for overcoming challenges. Exploring our purpose is not just based upon a career, but what we are built to do.

For years, I struggled with the idea that I did not fit in with my own family of origin. I grew up in an area where culture lent itself to poverty, lower education, and traditional roles and views of men and women. My family constitutes women as being caretakers, homemakers, and loyal to the men who provide. As I grew older, my voice and ideas became louder, and my points of view became less heard. I was not going with the grain of my family, but I was going with the grain of myself. Don't get me wrong, I have children, and I was pretty good and changing diapers, embracing my inner core of domestication by cooking, decorating, school projects, and putting the needs of others before myself. However, I knew that my purpose was not meant to serve as the women before me in my family had.

Family of origin, or as I will refer frequently in my words, the F.O.O. serves great influence to who we become. In my earlier years of practice, I worked with students in higher education who were faced with conflict of choosing a major. F.O.O. dictated that they would be lawyers, because simply put, all the other men or women in the family were lawyers. Therefore, that was the expectation. The problem was, they thrived in the bounds of art, creativity, expression, and although it may not have served the purpose of the F.O.O., it served deeply to who they were in their community. I related such as I was happy to become a mother, but I too had a greater task to fulfill my meaning of existence. I was meant to help. I was meant to find independence and utilize a voice far greater (although when my mother was angry, her yell was definitely heard!) than my F.O.O. had produced me to have. In point, becoming a healthy individual has to include owning your true talents and going with, not against the grain of your natural aptitude, desire, and purpose.

People, support systems, family members, and your community may not ever quite understand what it is you are set out to accomplish, but in most cases, they will remain loyal to the least extent of loving you anyway. Even if you end up as the black sheep of the circle. Again, it all comes back to owning it, owning you, owning your talents, and accepting not defending the natural talents you were born with.

At the age of 6, I remember waking up to the smell of coffee and overhearing voices coming from the news. Still dark out, I would listen to the sounds of the garbage man coming down the alley and the most annoying "singing" from the local Chachalaca birds during these humid summer mornings. I would creep out of my bed, quietly tip-toe down the hallway, and peak my head around the corner into the kitchen where my step-dad David went about his early routine of making lunches, putting on his brown work boots, and prepping for an intensely hot day on the farm. As my younger brother would follow close behind me, I would crawl up in my Garfield night gown and laugh at the tickle of his mustache as he kissed us both goodbye.

As a kid, the only thing I really understood was that my step dad was the coolest guy ever. He drove huge tractors, and sometimes let us operate the module builders during cotton season. On occasion, we were allowed to run out with him at night to deal with irrigation. I remember thinking he was a great hero and my brag moment was in the fourth grade when he came to speak to my class about farming because of some social studies thing we were doing.

In later adulthood, I learned more about the reality of farming. The cool equipment also meant uncool sacrifices. I never cared about money or anything beyond riding bikes in the neighborhood, which is probably why I never realized that we didn't have much money. Apparently farming is not the route to becoming wealthy. I also knew that my step dad was a really hard worker (I now call this work ethic); what I did not realize as a kid that I later understood is that he worked hard because farming is all he knew. He was born into a family farm and continued to work this career passed down from his FOO without really exploring other choices. I always figured my younger brothers would continue on with this legacy, but the farming eventually came to an end. The work ethic I grew up admiring however, is the real legacy that we all carry on.

FOO and Career have so many intertwined values that many of us never even consider. As I help individuals identify this part of their holistic identity, I often ask where their ideas for purpose come from or where they first learned about work and its meaning. As I reflect on the story of a farmer's daughter, I see the child describing her hero and the adult describing her learned value in providing for her family and taking pride in what she does.

Career choice is not only for the very smart or the incredibly rich, as many of my previous lower-income student clients may think. Career choice is built on an idea that we are capable of gaining insight and mapping out what we see as productive and valuable. Our FOO and natural abilities can be grown into talent, purpose, and daily self achievements. It may not always be validated or respected by our close circles of family and friends, but it is our small stamp on the world, and it is our opportunity for satisfaction, should we choose to explore it.

I don't know if my step dad ever found his purpose. I don't know if he had great moments of self reflection in those isolated tractor cabs on scorching summer days. I don't know if he realizes what his career identity ever was or could be. I do know that purpose is about intention, making the world better in some way, and if nothing else, he had a purpose that was indirect. His purpose may have been to show his family that life is hard, work is how to pay bills, and you do it everyday to show your kids you love them. Indirectly, perhaps his purpose was to teach me that perseverance and work ethic are good models for your kids so that one day they will go on to be a hero and leave a positive stamp in their world.

There are several resources to go about the career exploration part of Self. As a specialist in relationships, I tend to put a great emphasis on FOO, values, and culture. Systemically, understanding who you are by nurture helps to explain how you are built via nature. Nature is the basic premise of what your are born as versus nurture which is said to influence what you become. Both have equal contributions simply based on your unique perception of the odds you've been given and how you chose to work within those odds.

Personality tests are a great feature in career exploration and help us to articulate our strengths, skill sets, and offer categories that we may fit into based on these concepts. I would also agree that any part of career exploration should include spiritual reflection, astrological insights, and any resource that can provide us with some explanation as to why we like certain activities and how we can gain profit from them. Simply put, any tools or means by which we can gain a better understanding of Self can be useful in finding a healthy career and a meaningful purpose.

As we look at identifying and claiming this family centered explanation to how we gain Career Identity, what I would hope you would notice is that Self Exploration is naturally sprinkled into every part of this discovery. As we look at becoming a Healthy ME, it naturally makes sense to delve further into what Self Exploration can really look like.

Chapter 3: SELF EXPLORATION

In working with individuals, I still sit and work from a systems perspective. I never just see the individual in front of me. I see the voices, opinions, damages, pain, pride, and orientation of all these and more sitting on the couch beside them. I make it clear that when I work with an individual, as they bring in all of the challenges they've drowned in living life, that they need to see perspective on gaining real truth and leaving behind all that they have feared.

One of my favorite quotes is, "So many people in life will tell you can't, and all you have to do is turn around and say 'Watch Me.'" This quote means a lot to someone who has embraced their strengths, shut out the voices, and said "Fuck Off" or "love me as I am, quirks and all." It means so little to someone who isn't in a place of Self and personal acceptance. As I work with people everyday, I bring up words such as these, and the ultimate question is "How do I get there?" or "Where do I start?" My answer is always the same. Let's start with self exploration.

I'd like to paraphrase this as a client, but honestly, its just better to speak about truth with truth. This one is on me. FOO taught me well. It taught me direction, taught me to run from conflict and life, and most importantly, taught me to find my own direction. I spent my early 20's in school because it was the only idea I had that would rescue me from a life of empty solitude. I thought that going to school would absolve me of financial problems, domestic violence, neglectful parenting, alcoholism, and ignorance. I thought school and higher education would earn me acceptance as an adult-child seeking approval and love and more importantly, life-long unconditional love.

As all of us carry on the values that we interpret from our past, one thing we tend to look over is what foundation our values are built from and how they will stabilize us in our future. What may look like the idealistic way of leaving poverty and moving up to middle class or riches is what may also slap us later as a false interpretation of value. The childhood dream of becoming an actor turns into the legacy of becoming a politician with a white-picket fence. Our journey to abort the lifestyle of a farmer leads us to the detriment of slaving indoors 80 hours a week without windows. Self exploration is manipulated by interpreted meaning and is truly found by intrinsic motivation.

In my early 30's, I began the art of networking and utilized my natural talents, of what I coin as, "insta-friending" all who seem interesting. The term basically says that I never meet a stranger and attach quickly to people who are emotionally disconnected for entertainment.

As I socialized with my insta-friends (some last minutes, while others will be in my life forever), I started listening to stories of solo travels across the earth and brilliant ideas for inventions. What I once I thought was a productive decade of my early 20's suddenly became a regret of research papers and career oriented co-dependency. I had nothing to share in these conversations about far-off destinations, running with the bulls, or pig roasting. I could not relate to big family gatherings or holiday frustrations of airport crowds. I spent my 20's focused on one thing: Stability. And stability in my 20's meant emotional disconnect and futuristic ideals of escaping all that I knew. Stability meant taking what I learned growing up and following that direction or doing exactly the opposite to prove everyone wrong and to everyone that I could. Stability changes face though as we evolve into who we really are and our truth within self exploration catches up to us.

Oddly enough, my 20 something self had a better idea of truth when it came to meeting open and honest people. I had genuine people who wanted genuine lifestyles talk to me everyday. My 30 something self met people who were desperate in finding truth, learned I was easy to talk to, and ultimately were some of the most fake ambiguous bull shitter's I ever came across.

This is the turning point. This is when we

come to our crossroads of truth: I feel uneasy, certain there is more, and I am ready to own up to who I am, what I want, and dismiss this chaos that I thought was right for me. This is applicable to our relationships, jobs, loves, hates, and most of all, seeing truth in what is truly a good fit for us.

Self exploration is identifying what we know as normal and differentiating normal from what our intuition says fits us best. We accept "normal" for so long and experience inner turmoil and conflict to a point of incongruence. When we question it, we begin to find answers.

I worked with a client who was mandated to attend counseling for a few months. At our first meeting she had a good look to her; hair tied up neatly, work uniform for a fast food chain, detailed makeup, all accentuated with a black eye covered well and a busted lip shining with lip gloss. She was resistant at first, but after our first session, she was able to communicate the domestic violence issues she had experienced. She and her current partner were high school sweethearts. They had both come out around the same time and fell deeply in love. In high school, it was difficult for them to find people to connect to or share fears and sexuality. She came from foster care and years of being in the state system of custody. She went through sexual, mental, emotional, and physical abuse and saw love to be a distant privilege. Her partner came from a wealthy family who swept conflict and "dirty laundry" under the rug.

As we grew to know each other in sessions, I learned of her ideas about life, and what constituted a healthy relationship. Abuse was accepted because at least she knew that her partner would come home. She had a child as a result of a freshmen year incident where she (her interpretation) drank too much and didn't say "no" the right way. This child was part of why she stayed as well. Her partner was a strong provider and she did drink and party at home, but she provided the home, so it was worth the compromise. As we continued to work together, I assertively pointed out an idea: "Is it possible that you have normalized abuse as love?" She looked at me stern, pissed off, and grabbed a tissue for the first time in any of our sessions. As tears rolled down her face with anger and resentment, she looked at the clock, then up to the corner of the window, then back at me. She saw my statement as a reflection in a mirror and only had one response: "Does love come in any other way?"

This story has always stayed with me because every part of pain that we allow or accept comes with what we chalk up to "normal" for ourselves. Men who have proclaimed mommy issues accept being womanizers; women with sexual trauma act out promiscuity for instant gratification and love. There is no right or wrong, just a normal that we accept. Self exploration provides us with the insight that may lead to a better understanding of who we are, why we are, what we love and dislike, and what may come if we strive for it. The biggest component to a Healther ME is knowing the definition of ourselves. Definitions evolve and grow and are elaborate and honest. We explore who we are, how we came to be, and with this insight, possibilities of gaining the impossible are now within our reach.

Establishing a new "norm" in the process of self exploration begins with clarifying our perceived truths. As my client continued to explore where her truth of what love should look like, she also gained clarity into her own definition of what love could be that did not include so much pain and torment. Questioning what we know does have a catch — it puts us in a position of confusion and the need to replace this with better answers. I see this as one of the best parts in this journey, but it can be daunting and very liberating all in the same moment. As we gain clarity, we also gain open space to explore different options that seem better and more healthy for us.

A lot of people come to see me in practice because they are seeking some kind of change. Some would argue that people don't change. This is true for people who have no desire to change. Change happens when we want something different for ourselves and understand our individual drive and motivation.

As we go through the process of self exploration, I think its important to ask ourselves the right questions. Regardless of working with couples, children, or adults, I always emphasize never to ask WHY. If you ask why, people get defensive.

"Kennedy, why have you colored all over the wall?" My daughter, who was 3 at the time, is very clever. She looked up at me like, "yeah right, this is trap, and I'm not falling for it." Her expression was priceless and I had a lot of respect for it. So my better way of handling it the next time (yes, next time... she's my, um, very "independently expressive" child) was to say "Kennedy, you've made a picture on the wall... What is this a picture of?...Are colors used to make pictures on the wall?" She responded, only this time with some thoughtful explanation. She said, "No." She then went on to explain that colors are used for paper and she ran out of room on the paper so the wall was bigger to draw on. She then was able to have a one-on-one understanding with me about limits for coloring and it was the last of the coloring on the wall. Later in the parenting section, I may possibly bring up how this was followed by painting on the wall, but totally different tool used for drawing, so, yeah.

So if I'm speaking with a 3-year-old, 33-year-old, or an 83-year-old, I have learned to never ask Why. Too subjective. Who, What, When, Where, and How much or How long? These are productive staples when questioning "Who am I trying to become?" or "When did I decide I wanted more in life?" or "How long have I wanted to feel better?" and "Where was I when I was inspired to change this about myself." These are open-ended questions that lead to amazing answers for drive and motivation toward change and moving forward.

In specializing in relationships, I often focus on non-traditional dynamics and expand this in helping couples and individuals in the GLBT (Gay, Lesbian, Bisexual, Transgender) population. One of the greatest success stories I've had the pleasure in facilitating was with an individual who originally came to me hoping to address co-dependency patterns in his romantic relationships. As we went through the process of addressing self exploration and initiating ideas for what he considered what a Healthy ME would look like, we unveiled more truths than either one of us could have ever imagined possible.

In working with one of my transgender clients, the ideas of Healthy ME came to life on a level we both were eager to explore. Our work together began with this individual being a "she" in pronoun and biological sex; by sexual preference, attracted to women, and at this point, a self-identified lesbian. Throughout our working relationship, transition took place, so I clarify here that I refer in the pronoun of He.

"I have been a survivor my entire life. I have raised myself since I was a child, as my father was buried in work and my mother was M.I.A. in a world of drugs and unhealthy coping. I felt lost in the world and my only piece of identity that was certain was that I played the role of the protector to my younger siblings which then led me to always depend on needy relationships and sketchy work environments.

"I move around a lot because I have never felt safe in any environment and I have never felt secure in really knowing who I am. I came out as a lesbian early in high school but I felt like I had to hide it from my family so that I wouldn't disappoint them or create more drama than there already was. Now I am here in this new city in search of stability and getting to know who the real me is without having to explain myself to my family. I just ended a relationship with my girlfriend who I felt like didn't appreciate me. I did my best to take care of her and be a provider, but I still feel like I have been living a lie even when I was with her."

As we spent months creating road maps toward career, purpose, and ideas about what healthy relationships could look like, we came to a halt in therapy. After consistent appointments, occurring on the same day, same time, every week, he stopped and cut off all communication. I gave him a couple of weeks, thinking maybe things got busy at work. Eventually I reached out to him, concerned that maybe this abrupt halt came from something more than just needing a break in therapy.

Late one Tuesday night, I received a text message with a tone of desperation, clarity, excitement, and fear. He begged for the next available appointment time. Late in the evening that next day, he showed up immediately grabbed the box of tissue, and starred in silence at the rain falling outside my office window. After about 7 minutes of poised silence, he looked at me and began to break down.

"Savannah, do you think the trees feel better after it rains? Like, do you think that it washes away the impurities and lets them feel alive and organic again?" he asked.

After a long pause and some very intentional thoughts, he let me know that at this very moment, he was ready for self exploration and determined to focus on his new version of a Healthy ME. I asked one of the open questions to initiate where this motivation was coming from. I wondered if he felt ashamed in falling back into a codependent pattern with some girl and just didn't want me to feel disappointment towards him; I wondered if it might be worse and he may have considered giving up. I had a hundred thoughts within those few seconds, and in this next part of his story, I experienced with him an epiphany that lead to bravery, strength, truth, and acceptance of Self. In therapy we sometimes refer to this as a cathartic moment or the "Aha!" moment where you see the lights turn on in their eyes. And it was this moment that changed both of our lives in many different perspectives.

"Savannah, I was at work the other day and people were starring at me because they were confused about my gender," he said.

(Clarity: sex is the description of how you are biologically born; gender is how you choose to express your sex and sexuality).

"One of the people at work even called me on it. I get that I have short hair and wear boy clothes, but really? IT?! I walked around for hours downtown and came to a conclusion. It is not my role to protect the world from who I am. It is my role to let the world in and express who I really identify myself to be. I've been a boy my whole life. I've never felt more alive more sure and more confident that this moment right now. My greatest motivation for all this ME crap you keep telling me about was when I was labeled lower than a confused lesbian girl. When they called me an 'It,' I knew that it was time to stop hiding who I am and own my identity for all to accept," he said.

As we continued working together, we looked at all the concepts of his holistic identity and maintained that same motivation and drive-by addressing every possibility of what could be with bravery and intent. We conquered several phases of transformation in physical appearance, mental clarity, emotional security, relationships, and futuristic ideas for growth. Once he hit his moment for needing to find truth, he accepted himself, and that started a trend for allowing others to love and accept him as well.

This journey may not be relatable to everyone, but the concept of transition and seeking the truth to our holistic identity starts with one question: "What am I afraid of?"

"If I can start this part of my self exploration, will I be able to gain more control (and eventually, comfort, security, safety, and stability)?"

Chapter 4: FEAR

"I shut people out and never commit because I'm afraid of becoming a father. All relationships lead to children. I just don't have it in me to care for a kid. I never grew up with a father. He was around, but it was rare. When he was around, he was pretty drunk. As a kid, my brother and I would be sleeping in our bunk beds and I remember on school nights he would show up with his 'after party' and start blaring records of classic rock from the 'good-ole-days.' The drunk entourage would get lost on the way to the bathroom and pull us in to join the party. Sometimes it was kind of fun; crazy grownups dancing on furniture, my dad operating a martini shaker like a gambler operates a slot machine.

"Oddly enough, the sounds of those records somehow bring a level of peace to me now if I hear them at karaoke or tail-gate parties. I also just remember how angry my mom would get though. She would clean up the mess like it never happened, make us breakfast, and go on to work never showing an ounce of fear or sadness. She was strong and I always appreciated her for that, but I also saw her as weak for never leaving him. Once I left for college, I never looked back. They eventually split up, but there was never a connection built that I thought a father and son should have.

"I'm not going to lie, I like going out and drinks, drugs, and girls come with that. I also work hard and I work for what I have, but recently, I met this girl and I just all but snapped. She is different from everyone else. She has her shit together, good job, great smile. She's fun but serious, and really knows how to get me thinking. She's actually a keeper, but I pushed her away because she got too close, too personal, and made me too comfortable. I could talk with her for hours about work, life, nonsense, you know all the cool stuff the dumb ones can't keep up with. But she's on a whole different level and she deserves it all… marriage, kids… stuff that just scares the hell out of me."

Fear holds us back. It makes us second guess our logic and intuition. It stands in the way of our greatest accomplishments. And once we identify it, we can slap it in the face. Once it is revealed, it no longer holds power, because it is no longer scary to us.

I see this dilemma a lot with individuals who are unhappy in their relationships, in particular, the relationships they have with themselves. People disclose affairs to me but are unclear about how to end what feels happy and remain in what seems mundane. People hate their jobs but stay out of loyalty and fear of not being good enough to find a new one. People seek adventure and remain in the same five-block radius their entire lives. And in this case, an opportunity for a healthy connection is dismissed because it seems too perfect and real.

Fear is a major component in our holistic identity and plays a great role in defining a Healthy ME. I frequently say that the bottom line is this: People just want to feel safe and be heard. Fear jeopardizes our safety (whatever we think that looks like) and this is why it gets so much credit for being a component in our identity. Fear manifests from FOO, experience, rejection, and pain. Fear is also a coping skill as it is used in some ways to protect us from harm. To what extent though are we willing to dismiss insight and overlook this "protection" for what it really is and how much life it is blocking us from experiencing?

Through the process of finding a Healthy ME and committing to the journey of self explora-tion, a great place to start is by identifying fears and becoming educated about them. The more information we have on what it is that is hold-ing us back, the less afraid we are of it. Children are afraid of the dark and adults come in turn on the light, tour inside the closet, and show them the truth. It is not this simple though, at least not in my world. My imagination and thought process is far too stubborn to just take another adults kind words and perspective and suddenly stop being afraid. I can relate to children who don't trust simple explanations; the authorities who give them tend to have bad days too.

I see fear as two parts conditioned rationale and one part irrational. Based on what we've learned and experienced, these fears are somewhat built up on perceived truth. "If I live alone I could get robbed and raped… if I leave my job I might not find another one and end up homeless." The one part irrational holds more weight and depth, so if we are willing to break down what that fear is built on and how its validation came to be, we gain clarity. We become educated.

In continuing to work with this story of FEAR and creating ideas for growth, I reflect on this story where I saw a lot of opportunity in overcoming it by doing a simple breakdown of emotional disconnect and facilitating "education" so that if nothing else, he knew the difference in rational versus irrational thoughts.

If I consider my experiences from my dad and look at my life choices now, I see this as mostly rational because I think I might be a lot like him.

FEAR 1: "I don't want kids because I fear I am turning out to be just like my dad. He was a bad dad, so that means I will be a bad dad."

Response: You have insight that may lead you to see your role in parenting different from how your dad viewed his role. You may also consider how your life choices now may not be what they would look like if you had someone meaningful to spend time with.

"I think this girl is really amazing; but look at me. Why would she ever stay with someone like me? Let's say she does stay, she'll probably try to change my whole life and trap me."

FEAR 2: "I am not sure that I deserve a girl like this. I am not sure that she'll love me for me or that I'm good enough."

Response: It's tough to think that you might not have a clear perspective on what other people see in you. It's important to consider that you have a lot of qualities that draw people at your equal level in; and you have qualities that won't always push them out if you choose not too.

As we continued to breakdown some basic ideas behind the fears, it was more than just allowing him to work through fears. He was able to gain insight in to owning who he was and exploring options versus accepting the FOO curse he identified with. Something that I encouraged him to remember was that he was also half of his mom. He had a lot of good in him and although he may not have seen the whole picture as to how she made her choices to stay so long with what he considered a crap situation, he did need to see that her strength was also in him.

There are hundreds of situations that have crossed my path where life has lost its quality and the most obvious solutions seem impossible. Fear looks the same whether we talk about perceived success or failure. As I walk through unique scenarios, I frequently ask where the fear starts and begin a break down of what it truly means to the individual. Most of us are logical and see problems for what they are and go in search of simple solutions. The solutions however typically have a string of consequences that complicate the changes we are looking to make. We fear the unknown, and although we may not like the situation we are in, it is sometimes easier to stick with what is predictable rather than chasing something outside of our routines.

In my practice, I created a little "Business Practices 101" outline that helps counselors (and really anyone who wants to become more enterprising) see past the fear of failure in starting a private practice. I acknowledge the basic fears of financial stress, competition or saturation of therapists in the market, and most importantly, their fear of quality within their specialties.

This little workshop outline was not created from thin air. True, it has some merit because I stepped far out of my own comfort zone and field and started doing a lot of research by self educating based on my own fears. I read several books on entrepreneurial practices, finance strategies, marketing, and corporate leadership. I often joke that although I was my father's greatest disappointment by not pursuing an undergraduate degree in business, I did assist in 75 percent of my best friend's BBA. Ultimately though, it is a valuable tool because it is written based on making more mistakes than I care to remember and taking more risks than I think most people's ego can tolerate. My 20 something fear of living a life without stability lead to my late 20 something thriving on chaos. My fear was my greatest motivator in exploring just how much I could lose, get rejected, fail, and ultimately discover how much more I wanted to offer the world.

So I sort of get it. I get that jumping into a business or a relationship can be really intimidating if we feel like we don't have the knowledge or means to make it succeed. My real fear in life though is never failing because I was never willing to try.

Fear is a gift. It takes energy and will. It is our greatest asset in self exploration, understanding who we are, and its a gift that keeps on giving. Fear never ends. As we continue the journey to discovering a Healthy ME, we have be totally okay with the fact that the more we seek truth in ourselves, the more fear we could gain. As I see it, this means there is a plethora of opportunity for more growth to occur and learning just how awesome things can really be.

Going through any transition during exploration is admirable and courageous. As we identify fears and gain insight to what healthy growth can be, we also become more driven to never let go of this new freedom. Letting go of what the world thinks is an amazing form of liberating the soul, personal spirit, and holistic self. As clients work through transitions of letting go of insecurities and embracing their true forms of self, they also need to consider how they will continue to stay strong and cope with everyday adversities. Working with people in transition is a constant reminder of how important it is to make time for self reflection, time for process, and the most significant idea of the Healthy ME: Self Care.

Chapter 5: SELF CARE

Eagles singing in the background, chicken sizzling in the pan, a tall glass of 512 IPA (yes, many of you are wine connoisseurs, I am the white-trash class of beer connoisseurs), peace is in the silence of my thoughts, my cooking, my imagination running wild, and endless love of from the lyrics playing that I am in my true form of self. I am in my ambiance of self care.

I worked with a client and I'll never forget our first meeting. We were discussing some of her life's trials and tribulations, and as I piece together some solutions, I ask her what she does in her daily routine that is just for her. She honestly looked at me with confusion and said, "Why would I need to do that?" I found myself in the wrong chair in the office. I was puzzled, speechless, confused, and honestly, stuck. I could not wrap my head around the idea that this brilliant, beautiful, and articulate woman sitting across from me had questioned the idea of self care! As we continued our session, I began to jot down some ideas for homework so she could continue her self reflection. I asked her to write down, on one side, things she could find to do each day for herself that only she could benefit from, and on the opposite side, things she thinks she is doing for herself, but how other people in her life are actually benefiting.

As a compliant and studious client, she returned the next week with the homework completed, but she felt more resentful and less at ease than expected from leaving her previous session. As I began to engage in these unexpected feelings she presented, I learned this. She could not think of one thing she did in a day that solely benefited her. Everything she did was to appease or take care of her children, husband, school obligations, work, or neighboring friend. Even the concept of exercise stemmed back to her mother ridiculing her for letting her body "go" and lead to her concerns about an aging body that her husband would no longer find attractive. The meals she prepared always took into account the dietary preferences of her family. Even shopping was dictated by how her work colleagues would perceive her sense of style and power. Every daily activity was geared toward pleasing the idea of another, and to her dismay, there was no reward in the end. She could not place how and why this came to be.

In later sessions, I had to "own" where I initially made a mistake. She had not addressed where her stress came from. She felt so beat up by failure to make progress in these sessions; and really, I overlooked where I needed to meet her on all three levels. She was not able to comprehend self care because she was not ready. Setting the ground work for truly embracing self care begins with gaining clarity in the areas of life we feel challenged. I wish it were as simple as finding a hobby or overcoming the fear of looking selfish. But just as all of the other components of a Healthy ME are broken down, the component of self care follows suit.

Self care needs to be addressed in three forms: Physical, mental, and emotional. I specify this separation based on the idea that stress also appears in these three forms. In order to truly be ready and capable of making progress during this journey of self exploration, the constituents of stress need to be reflected on so that maintaining our health through self care mirrors its cause and effects.

In coming from a theoretical perspective of positive Psychology, I seek answers by helping clients see where their current strengths exist and how their current challenges are blocking these resources and tools. Simply put, challenges are overcome by strengths and strengths are what initiate self care and daily maintenance of a Healthy ME.

Stuck. This is the word used to best describe that limbo feeling of helpless, hopeless, impossible confusion. It can resemble feelings of depression and anxiety all at once. It is also the breaking point where we can step back and use logic to figure out how we feel challenged and where we need to start paying attention to ourselves. I use an annoying little saying, "Can't be a healthy (parent, partner, worker…) without being Healthy ME first." This also is where we look at what we are doing right and where we are failing to listen to our bodies. This is where solutions and ideas for self care come from.

Physical Stress

I felt as though I was suffocating in this daily ritual we call life. I love my kids and they are my most significant reason for existing. They give me purpose and make me laugh. They define my perspective of balance, meaning, and the will to always strive to be better. But as much as I love them, they exhaust me. Between school drop offs and pickups, bath time, home-work, making three-square meals plus snacks, and diffusing arguments, I'm spent. As I gave one last kiss, and offered one last sip of water during one of our bed time routines, I started to feel my breathing pacing faster and a sense of panic rushing through me. I turned off the light, set the timer for the white noise machine, and walked straight out to the back patio, where I experienced a major physical, emotional, and mental melt down.

Physical stress exhausts our energy and can appear in forms of lethargy, appetite change, anger, and panic attacks. It is the more concrete reaction to stress and our bodies let us know when it has had enough. Think of a bottle of soda. If you shake it up while it's already bottled under pressure, and you don't slowly remove the cap to let small amounts of pressure out at a time, it will explode.

Knowing what I was physically experiencing, I started to consciously slow down my breathing, address my thought patterns by talking to myself out loud, and gain my composure in returning to a place of "stable." Practicing slow breathing, stretching my limbs, and vocalizing my pressured thoughts was only going to help with the physical reaction to the stress my body was experiencing. I knew it would come back though if I did not take some time to regroup and address what the real cause was. Emotionally, it was time to do a self check and listen to how this physical stress was triggered.

Emotional Stress

Emotional stress is accumulated from multiple experiences that we have not allowed our brains to process. In a world that is cut throat, fast paced, and futuristic in thinking, it does not always allow for time to address every little negative emotion or dislike we experience. So, in the moment of distress, our brains have a way of compartmentalizing these negative emotions. In most cases, as life goes on, we forget to "clear out the junk drawer" and the storage in our brains becomes packed, so emotionally, stresses start to seep out, and usually at the most random and inopportune times. The pattern to pay attention to here is what triggers these emotional stresses. Sometimes if we continue to dismiss these triggers and stresses for long amounts of time, or in this case, years, it becomes too much and we have to go back to where it started in order to put it to rest.

I examined patterns of emotional stress surrounding the beginnings of my parenting career. Going as far back to when my husband and I decided to have kids (or more like found out one was on the way), I reflected on where some of my dismissed compartmentalizing started. We had to have that talk about adjusting finances and looking at work schedules so we could provide care in the way we preferred. I chose to take a break from my full-time job and stay home to focus on our first daughter. After about 6 months of being sleep deprived from a colicky baby, I felt like going back to work part-time would help me regain balance.

About a month after taking the step toward working on my professional identity and getting the swing of balancing nursing and pumping, I found out that baby No. 2 was on her way. I literally stared at this drug store stick mocking me with a football-stadium sized bright red plus sign, and then looked down at my daughter who was mastering the tasks of crawling and holding her own bottle.

Owning up to my naivety of being a super

human in my mid-20s, I can pinpoint where I started neglecting myself. The birth of my second daughter arrived in some bitter-sweet circumstances. I was in the middle of a job transition, financially uncertain about where this transition would lead me, and focused on completing my licenser hours. I was also denying some grieving that was well overdue after arriving at the one-year anniversary of my grandmother's death. My thriving 18-month-old angel was now a big sister, that I felt like I was neglecting so I could nurse her even more colicky little show stealer. In an attempt to keep up with the developmental needs of both babies, I stayed home with them during the day, and worked evenings, nights, and weekends. Talk about spent.

One more piece to add to this pattern was the overlooked fact that my work consisted of the most stressful therapy I have ever provided in my life. Leaving a newborn and almost toddler at home, I would provide services with at-risk young parents fighting depression, poverty, abuse, all while attempting to care for their own babies. The pattern I picked up on during this mini self intervention of emotional stress was this: I had no time to slow down and even less time to address all the ways I was giving but not receiving.

Mental Stress

Sitting on my back patio, looking seriously crazy I'm sure to my neighbors, I vocalized out loud to myself the emotional stresses I had never addressed. I'd like to think that crying is just a version of sweating during an emotional workout. Heaven forbid I should give up my title of being superhuman. As the emotions seeped out during this cathartic night, I gained clarity and depth into what I needed to address with logic and rationale.

Mental stress is this form that wreaks havoc on our rational thinking, cognitive functions, and organization of logic. I was at a point where I could start to clarify my thoughts and perceptions, and start building up a plan that was organized, productive, and quite frankly, more truthful than I really wanted to admit.

The emotional stress that had built up over my second daughter's first year of life eventually conquered me in the form of mental stress. It was only now, in this midst of this mid-night melt down that I gained clarity of myself, where I was personally responsible for being unhealthy, and ultimately where and when I had to own my part in ending a marriage and making the choice to enter single parenthood. I found my place in what was my present and I was ready to sort through my mistakes, my current triggers, and find some inner peace so

I could get my head out of my ass and accept that I was, in fact, not a super human. I was just human.

My suffocation came from basically lying to myself through use of self justification for making questionable and perhaps regretful choices. Dwelling on mistakes is never productive, and knowing this I quickly took my mental clarity and turned it into a truthful learning experience. In exploring my emotional patterns, I recognized that I pride myself in being strong and showing pain makes me look weak. I started by challenging this thought and gaining a new perspective. The truth in my being strong comes from focusing on what I can control and what I cannot. I can control my schedule, who I say "yes" to, and owning when I need to ask for help. I learned from this challenge that I should have given credit to my husband for having his own strengths rather than assuming I had to carry the strength alone and be solely responsible for myself and my children. I also learned that relinquishing control allows for a lot more positive energy rather than maintaining a one-sided view point. He may have had a very different perspective on life and family, but ultimately, I created my own stress by missing the bigger picture of having love within a family instead of just focusing on how to provide for a family.

Another pattern I recognized was how I

dismissed my FOO and followed my fears of falling into a trap of instability and only saw one solution. To run. I challenged this thought by looking at how running only added more stress to my life rather than escaping it. This daily ritual of life that included parenting alone, managing a career, and attempting personal gain would have been significantly easier had I been open to more than my one learned perspective. This learning opportunity taught me to see that even though my husband and I were very opposite in career expectations and professional goals, it did not mean that his good heart and kindness would lead to poverty. Perhaps it would have lead me in another direction or not, but either way, I continued to explore the truth in my mental stressers and started to outline my plan for taking back control of my stress and evaluating how to take care of ME.

Creating a Plan for Self Care

If you ask anybody what my best friend is in session, they would say "The Legal Pad." It is a simple way to organize thoughts, concrete, and visible. Self care begins with drawing a line down the middle of a legal pad and on one side writing "Strengths" and on the other writing "Challenges." Intentionally, I use the word challenges rather than weaknesses. Weakness implies we don't have control over changing this, where as, challenges are obstacles that can be overcome using our strengths.

As I make a list of my strengths, I include all the strengths that make up my holistic identity: Professional, educated, driven, giving, loving, ….and so on. Under "Challenges," I list out what I would like to see as better, easier, or capable of improving. This may include breaks from making lunches at night, reorganizing financial priorities, exploring old hobbies and discovering passions. I consider these "Challenges" because clearly, based on the mini breakdown, I was not doing any of these for myself.

As I considered my "Strengths," I then asked how I could use these on myself in addition to giving them out to others. As I evaluated my "Challenges," I started linking my "Strengths" to help me plan responses and behavioral actions to make my "Challenges" improve. I get that I don't have a magic wand, and I hate to admit that. So in the mean time, I can say that my passion for cooking, listening to music I like versus preschool songs, and finding meaningful ways of expressing my emotions seem to help me take care of ME. I find joy in making art and hanging it up in my room where it is simply good enough for me to look at (and cuts out the burden of worrying about what other people think about it). Some people express themselves through gardening, journaling, singing, kayaking… the possibilities are endless. It just takes some time to explore what the "thing" is that drives your passion and releases energy that could potentially get trapped in that junk drawer part of your brain.

Self care is not selfish. It is a necessity that allows us to self reflect, process out negative emotions, think clearly, and ultimately give to the world in the ways we desire.

I still remain busy, so part of my own organization is to schedule time for self care just as I schedule time for appointments, sessions, paying bills, and running errands. I continue balance my life in a way that enables me to unleash the healthiest form of myself that I can offer. Overall, my mandated time to focus on building a Healthy ME benefits all of the components to my holistic identity. I am a happier parent, more thoughtful therapist, less guilty ex-partner, and confident individual who will continue to thrive in chaos by choice, not default.

Chapter 6: SUMMARY OF HEALTHY ME

Why is it necessary? What will it lead me to? How will I know I've become more healthy? These questions are examples of knowing you are ready for the next step. It reminds me of taking an algebra class as an undergrad. I felt so lost and confused, so when the professor asked if we had any questions, I remained clueless and silent. Once I grasped some concepts and took time to learn about what we were working on, I knew enough to ask the right questions and explore the steps to gaining the right answers. Although life is not a mathematical formula with black and white answers, it can feel complicated and equally intimidating as a college-level math class.

Evolving and exploring a Healthy ME allows for two important concepts. First, we are comfortable with living in our own skin, hearing and expressing our own thoughts, and asserting ourselves in the many facets that play into our holistic identities. Being alone feels less lonely. Making decisions becomes simplified and eliminates some of our internal conflict with second guessing our logic and intuition. We are free and have only opportunity for growing into a better version of ourselves every day for the rest of our being.

Second, we are ready to share ourselves openly with partners who compliment our strengths and accept our quirks. A Healthy ME can describe what they would like in a partnership and feel comfortable in distinguishing what once felt like rejection from understanding who is and is not a good fit. It is always a continuation of process and insight, but as humans, we are built to coexist in cohorts with other people and thrive in companionship. Maybe it comes from our survival instincts as one-time cavemen and we're just trying to survive being eaten by a dinosaur. But either way, we live longer more healthy lives when we are not in isolation.

Healthy ME has the skills and tools to see people clearly for who they are and in turn, work together toward a lifestyle of healthy relationships. Partnerships come from this premise: Common interests are shared, an acquaintanceship is formed, as time builds trust and friendship evolves, then respect develops into best friendships. Once a mutual sexual chemistry is established, best friends become romantic and discuss healthy expectations for commitment and futuristic ideals. As two Healthy ME's come together to form this partnership, they evolve into what the second part of this book explores: a Healthy US.

PART II: HEALTHY US

Chapter 7: HEALTHY US DEFINED

Healthy US is this: Show up each day by choice, not obligation.

Just as in exploring and creating the components that go in to a Healthy ME, we have to look at the beauty and chemistry it takes to create and thus maintain a Healthy US. We react and evolve in patterns. In a session with partners who are coming for premarital counseling or intervention for infidelity, they all do one thing the same; they show me 90 percent of their story within 60 seconds or less using nothing but non-verbal communication. It is odd because if I point out this obvious language, they tense up, sometimes laugh, and then when I tell them that this is exactly how they became and US to begin with, their eyes fill with intrigue. My famous line is this, "Tell me how you met." I'm not listening to the context or mutual connection they laugh through; I'm listening to the initial basic first impression and the non-verbal expression that comes alive in front of me as though we have traveled through time.

"I met one of her colleagues at a networking event. I was working on some PR campaigns and thought we could possibly benefit each other. About a week later, I touched base via email and arranged a meeting with her. We agreed to meet for coffee to discuss some ideas and explore what each other had to offer. Had it been set up as a first or blind date, I may have put some thought in to what I would wear or at least feel one or two butterflies just because the expectation of 'awkward' would be possible. This was business; I was unarmed, ill prepared, and ready to talk shop.

"I got to the coffee shop a few minutes later than scheduled. I didn't know what she looked like but you can usually tell who it is as they look up every time someone new walks in the door. So, I walked in, didn't see her, and ordered my drink. I thought maybe she was running late so I just sat down at a table and figured I'd give it a couple of minutes. As I sat down and started looking over email, this beautiful woman caught my eye. She was wearing this coral colored dress and had her hair just laying really natural and easy. Her eyes stood out from the sunlight gleaming in from the window. As I caught myself staring, I sort of shook my head, and grinned to myself going back to my emails. About a minute later, she came up to my table, put out her hand and introduced herself. It was her. This was my business meeting! I thought she would be a lot older and less attractive based on how her colleague looked and described her personality and experience. But no, there I was ill prepared and taken back; completely unarmed. She never looked away from me and I couldn't take my eyes off of her smile and the way she moved her hands when she got excited about different ideas. I just knew; she was someone I wanted to be with."

Non-verbal communication is so important in looking at how a Healthy US us developed. We initiate interest with elongated eye contact and putting our hands behind our head. As we get to different levels of intimacy we adjust our hips and clinch our fingers to let our partners know how we are feeling and what we are thinking. A Healthy US begins in a mutual, non-verbal dialect that symbolizes validation, respect, and trust.

As we explore how a core foundation of a Healthy US is established, maintained, and or reconciled, I try to consider the strengths that were always present from the beginning and facilitate insight into how they have evolved or where they can be explored if they were missed at some point in the early phases of the relationship.

A Healthy US defined is actually so simple and yet so undefinable. In simplicity, it is a system of two individuals who share common interests, enjoy effortless companionship and ideas with each other, and ultimately work through any differences upholding the values of respect and trust. More simple than this is really the concept of showing up each day by choice. This implies that if situations are difficult or easy, they are valuing you as a partner and choose to keep you in their life. Obligation may come from traditional ideals and monetary stipulations, but the only obligation a Healthy US should focus is on is that of understanding and support of one another's perception of being a Healthy ME.

Chapter 8: COMMUNICATION

Couples often come to me seeking a better way of communication. They assume that this means more talking or talking using better language. Much to their dismay, my first response is not the typical "I statements" or a standard definition of good and bad communication. I actually start with one main phrase, "You have two ears and one mouth, so listen twice as much as you speak." Candidly, I encourage couples to realize from each other that the greatest gift of communication is the willingness of being completely present and in the moment, offering only that of listening and truly hearing what their partner is trying to say.

Although this may sound simple, it is perhaps the best kept "secret" to making any relationship work. If you think about it, most of the time when we're having conversations, we're trying to come up with our next response or a solution to the information we are picking up on. The idea of silence and filling the gap of what could be perceived as a moment of awkwardness is actually taking away from the opportunity for clarification and processing.

Offering the true act of hearing is a gift. It says, "I am present and in the moment listening with intent and trying to understand where you are coming from." This is not an act of thinking about what you are going to say next or preparing with your defense statement. It is simply hearing out what your partner is trying to say and nothing more. It is not agreeing with them. It is not about who will win this power struggle. It comes from a place of respect.

Tools that I like to use for healthy communication all create an atmosphere for a neutral playing field.

Hi/Lo: This is useful for sharing and venting highlights of the day. Some days are really great and we have a hundred "Hi's" to share. Some days are super crappy and all we can talk about is all the disappointments and devastations we experienced. So the rule to the Hi/Lo is that each partner gets one "Hi" and one "Lo." On a great day the "Lo" can be something silly like wishing they could have slept in 10 minutes more. On a crappy day, the "Hi" can be as basic as putting on clean underwear. There is no need to pressure either partner to fix or offer solutions to the Hi/Lo. It is just an opportunity to share and possibly exchange validation or support.

Naming the Ideals: Each partner can create a list of three things they like and are seen as functional. On the opposite side, they can put down three ideals which can symbolize were they feel challenged or what they would like to see different. A time and place for discussing the lists is negotiated. Then, each partner takes a turn describing one item off of each side of the list. In return, the other partner can ask for clarification if they do not understand the item or they can offer validation by saying how they too want that and agree to discuss how to implement steps toward gaining the ideal.

Basic "heads up": Schedules can get busy with errands, meetings, kids, and business trips. So in some moments, we may feel stressed or insecure about something and seek comfort from our partner. Ranting texts and multiple voicemails tend to shut down communication opportunities. So a basic "heads up" can do one of two things: 1. A simple statement of seeking comfort when available, but not an emergency. 2. Asking your partner if now is a good time to talk or ask if they have a minute. This assertive way in asking permission to speak allows mental and emotional preparation for partners to give the requested attention and avoids miscommunication of not caring or devaluing.

Communication is not only verbal. Some of the most significant forms of communicating as we've explored, are non-verbal. Sometimes just sitting next to your partner or bringing in a cup of tea as a gesture of support can be more effective that coming up with the right words to say. Non-verbals are very intimate and show sincerity. It also adds an element of affection and appropriate space for partners to sort through there own issues before bringing them into the

US unit.

Communication has a variety of patterns and disclosures. Every Healthy US will have different styles of communicating needs, wants, feelings, and emotions. If approached with respect and trust, the need for defense subsides. Discussions that inspire and entertain us like politics, culture, futuristic fantasies, and hope can become effortless and enhance intimacy. Communication is productive, informative, and full of quality as each of you has the luxury of having each other to share life's adventures with. Basically, its an opportunity to appreciate that you have someone significant to, well, just talk too. And this appreciation is invaluable and can sustain a lifetime of a Healthy US.

Chapter 9: SEX AND SEXUAL COMMUNI-CATION

Sex

The sun light is peaking through my gray curtains. I'm warm, cozy, unsure of the day or time; I don't care. My alarm never went off and that means one thing; today is mine to do as I please. I can splurge on chocolate chip pancakes. I can bask in the comfort of minimal clothing. I can drink coffee or forget to make it and have a mimosa. The best part about what I am waking up to is this - I am responsible for one thing and one thing only, looking to my left, adoring the human beside me, embracing the glow of the skin being kissed by first sunlight, grasping for the warmth of the shoulder that lay beside me. I have one duty to fulfill and it only includes falling madly and insanely in love today with the person I've chosen as my partner.

Sex is a subjective topic, and it should be! However, sex is so much more than the act of intercourse and orgasms. It's everything. Sex is vulnerability that embraces pleasure. Sex is personal expression, individually and shared. Sex includes conversation, physical touch, spiritual exploration and above all, it's the one component that separates the US relationship from every other relationship in our lives.

Naked Couch Sunday

It's the day of rest. The day of recovery from the fun Saturday night out downtown. It's the day the grandparents decided to take the kids out for ice cream and a movie. It's the day we share one couch, watch movies and catch up on our favorite series of shows, and it's the day of relentless sex, nakedness, and vulnerability. We don't need clothes, we don't need conversation, we don't need money, we don't need to do work, check emails, do laundry, or cook. We order Chinese delivery and pizza. We live by a pillow, a throw blanket and quilt, and time is the essence of our being one. It is the definition of the total trust, magic, and untouchable peace within and of us. This day is not tainted with the need to resolve issues There is no place for insecurities to seek reassurance. All there is to it is comfort, touch, soft forehead kisses, gentle hair strokes, occasional giggles and whispers, possible commentary to the idiot actors on the screen, but most of all, it is full of intimacy at its deepest core.

I spoke at a Contemporary Couples Conference one Spring, and while my topic was based on enhancing intimacy and affection, the audience was in disbelief as well as intrigued as I opened with this story. I painted the picture that many see a fantasy and not as the thread that differentiates their partnerships as a consummate relationship. The idea of the US is created from love, passion, trust and respect. More bluntly put, best friends, hot sex, amazing orgasms, lust, desire, shared fears, shared tears, and the strength to get through anything as long as the US operates on these premises. No, I'm not making this up. I'm not an idealist. I'm not even sure that the "marriage license" piece of paper belongs in this category. But what I am sure of is this: The couple that enters my therapy office, full of curiosity, hope, doubt, and trust is the couple that yells, cries, screams, speaks before thinking, laughs, and above all, shares my couch as though I've placed them in a folding chair. They are the couple with raw genuine challenges who have the "thing" that I cannot facilitate. They have passion, will, and the foundation to make their story carry on.

Working with couples is a very unique territory because the US has a culture that has been created. Two individuals have combined their idiosyncrasies that have cultivated a very protected foundation. It's as though they've fused together two personalities that also incorporate their irrational thoughts, magnificent strengths, and sideways expectations. When I ask them what sex looks like as a component in their relationship, I brace myself for what answers are to come. The culture of the unique US may include swinging, pornography, scheduled sex, and basic rules and roles that are typically unspoken habits that in very significant ways define how the sexual relationship unveils.

Healthy human sexuality encompasses multiple aspects that actually begin in early childhood and continue into individual adolescent and adult development. Going back to the Healthy ME concepts, it is important to do individual self exploration within the sexual component of the holistic identity. Parents often ask me when its appropriate to begin the discussion of sex with their kids. With sincere honesty, I give them my very direct answer, which usually results in wide eyes and a jaw drop.

As soon as someone announces they're expecting, the first question is whether it will be a boy or a girl. By definition, this is asking what the sex of the baby is going to be. Culture begins to market while we are in the womb so we stock up on diapers with butterflies or baseballs, rush out to grab everything pink or blue, and so it begins! The birth happens, and where I'm from, we pretty much rush from the hospital to the mall to push tiny diamond studs in their ears, because heaven forbid someone mistake are little princess for a boy!

When my children were babies, I participated in a little group of new moms who came together in support of each other. We would swap tips and make recommendations based on what we were learning. Stories were shared of sleepless nights, circumcisions, the terrors of what really happens during birth, and I won't even start on the breastfeeding truths! One afternoon at a "pump and dump" barbecue (quick reference: pump the milk and dump it so dad can take over and mommy can enjoy a margarita), one of the mom's shared a funny story about a diaper run adventure she had with her son.

As they were strolling through the isles, she had a baby in the cart and her older son, who was about 3-years-old, wandered off into the rolling racks of clothes. As she walked up to grab his hand, she discovered it was preoccupied while his little eyes lit up in amazement and his lips pierced in a pleasant state of curiosity. All of the parenting books she studied so hard completely escaped her memory as she reacted like many mommy's would in surprise! With a shout, a gasp in air, and an attempt to hide her giggle with tears, she yanked the preoccupied pleasuring hand as she faced her first experience in putting a stop to this little in-discrepancy of early masturbation.

Just to clarify, kids understand that masturbation is a normal part of discovering their bodies. A penis is just as exciting as finding a tongue or a belly button. Pleasure from masturbating is equivalent to pleasure from eating chocolate cupcakes. So in assisting this normal process of human growth and development, parents are encouraged to remove any stigmas from their sexual education and focus on being supportive during all phases of the process.

As we grow into our own selves, we learn more about sexual differences, gender identity, and what we feel is comfortable in our individual human sexuality. Evolving into a healthy sexual partner should include basic insight into what sex means to us, how we feel comfortable expressing pleasure, where are ideas of meaning come from, and of course, the subconsciously planted preconceptions from our FOO. I'm not ignorant to the fact that sex happens. It's hot. It's awesome and in the heat of arousal, nobody really gives a shit about any of this. I am also not referring to quick impulsive sex or the one night stand. Both have their time and place in sexual experiences, but again, I'm referring to the really great sex that evolves between two partners who just seriously get each other's needs, wants, desires, and triggers (not stress triggers but the good kind of triggers).

Naked Couch Sunday can be amazing, but a little bit of ground work needs to be set up before that can happen. The vulnerability it requires is so beyond the menial bar charm and cheap beers. At times, we accept what the bar talk may give us. Fun, excitement, something new and unconquered. Sexual vulnerability though is created from intense passion founded by trust, respect, intimacy and friendship. As I describe this to couples who are seeking "spice" or a rekindling in their neglected sex life, I sense of lot of resistance. The quick bar talk may hold the threat of rejection, but really, my fear of it is part of the bigger picture. At then end of an expensive bar tab and a quick fling, there may be some superficial cuddling and possibly a next time, but more so than not, it was just that - a quick fling. What is really left over is not an eight-hour marathon of orgasms, tears, terms of endearment, or even food delivery; it's really just a day of feeling hungover in an empty bed. So when I talk to couples about sex and how to make it better, I revert back to the Healthy ME concepts of fear. Fear holds us back. Rejection stems from fear. The process of finding the balance between finding the "quick and dirty fling at a bar" and a partner who is an amazingly "good fit" is by identifying truth, understanding individual fears, and openly communicating comfort levels that all lead up to Orgasmic Vulnerability. It is the healthy answer to avoiding rejection.

So a girl walks into a bar (and yes this a classic intro to a joke, but just come along with the adventure). It's her birthday and she's celebrating a decade past 24. She canceled her entire Tuesday to celebrate; and this comes from her subconscious FOO who has taught her that birthdays trump any government or religious holiday. With an open mind, and appreciation of the great sun, a pretty good hair day, and a beautiful fitted-short dress, she sat for a moment and realized how empty she felt inside. Looking around at the obvious surroundings, it became too difficult to see that her mature perspective of independently celebrating her birthday really meant that she was sitting alone at a bar, mid afternoon on a Tuesday ... on her birthday. Her FOO, who instilled this birthday culture, is dead. Physically, mentally and spiritually. She thinks for a minute, regains focus on her certainty and confidence, and without her usual preconceived plan of action, starts to enter a comfort zone that will forever make her question original logic, reason, and the need for remaining in control.

She accepted her drink, and being one of three patrons on this sunny afternoon, she engaged in conversation with a very attractive person sitting near her. His eyes were mysterious and yet filled with kindness. Something about the tone of his voice evoked this gut wrenching reaction almost as though she became spellbound. As they continued to participate in small talk, his intellect became obvious and typical deal breakers turned in to the charm of the deal makers. Just being in his presence made her feel irregular breathing and all experiences of logic and reason were suddenly forgotten.

If I were telling this story in my Psychology class, I would interject some facts to explain some of this woman's reactions. In addition to a strong serotonin imbalance from her recent disappointing birthday dinner, the sudden burst of oxytocin released from this sexual attraction may be exacerbated and extreme. I may also touch base on how her physical responses include dilated pupils, signifying subconscious stimulation and possible "gut wrenching reactions" to be explained by some technical endocrine system hormones. Now as much as I would like this to be a descriptive psycho-educational read versus a sexual fantasy novel, I can't adhere to text book explanations. Text book terminology is great for understanding the logical explanations to this story. But, sexual vulnerability is more about emotional reaction and passion. In other words, this is the "thing" that just needs to happen and evolve. Forget logic, this is passion.

As weeks went by, a friendship developed between them and small talk quickly turned into deep intimate conversations only trust can allow. The combination of intense sexual chemistry, intellectual stimulation, and mutual sharing of affection led to a sexual bond that encompassed erotic exploration and emotional bonding. There was no hesitation in sharing laughter or suggesting preferences, likes, and dislikes. There were no insecurities about lights being on or off or scheduling the sex around a certain time of day or night. Both partners relinquished all power and control and simply engaged in raw sexual emotions, thus exposing true forms of self through vulnerability.

Sexual vulnerability is a very powerful expression because it strips away any negative connotations that culture, society, history, or FOO integrate in the sexual experience. Ideas of guilt and promiscuity are obsolete. Anxieties from body image, labels, and performance become extinct. In allowing sexual vulnerability, there is one identifying factor that makes such ease of passion flow freely - Sexual Communication.

Sexual Communication

Sexual communication is derived from healthy forms of regular communication. This is why friendship and open dialogue is so important in experiencing great sex (and great orgasms). Sex happens all the time between strangers and may not include any communication. It can be good or at least satisfying. It is definitely a step above the truthful experience of drunk sex. But we are not talking about sex that is just okay or satisfying. This is a kind of sex that is shared in a Healthy US established by investing listening skills and the observation of verbal and very non-verbal communication. It occurs when you know your partner better than they know themselves and perform selfless acts of pleasure to ensure a combination of affection, emotional connection, and a very intense workout.

Sometimes I'll have a client contact me and remain completely ambiguous about their reason for scheduling an appointment. In this case, I guess I got busy into sessions, I responded to a muddled voicemail seeking couples counseling for "sex stuff" and I responded via text saying I would be able to coordinate a session. Moments after my acknowledgment of the message, I got a response asking for the earliest available appointment open that week. Not thinking much of it, I scheduled them in the calendar and walked in blind to what I was about to provide services for.

This couple in particular came in to see me and it took more bravery than any other couple I have ever met. They had survived the Vietnam War, four children, three grandchildren, challenges of addiction, some occasional verbal abuse, and now live the life of becoming travel companions and role models of marriage, except for one thing: He had the expectation for a sexual relationship to the point of exploring outside sexual relationship or divorce, and his partner was not willing to discuss or reciprocate.

The thing about younger couples and individuals is that they typically still have grandparents alive, and that means age is later, sex is now, and expectations are not realistic. Truth be told, the here is now, and the future is built on how we see ourselves as vulnerable, willing, and committed to exploring who we are, today. I always describe great sex and affection in the simplest manner: Great communication leads to great sexual communication, and great sexual communication leads to mind-blowing sex.

So often I meet people in the phase of exploring their own sexuality. Age is never a factor in this topic. I speak on this topic with 18-year-olds who are discovering their gender alliance and 50-year-olds who are dating and mating for the first time in 30 years. It always comes down to knowing yourself, knowing your past, and accepting what you see as a good fit for you. In most sessions, it's more about validating one's sexual exploration or processing the agony of sexual exploitation. So many partners and yet having the one get so good at it.

In the entirety of their marriage, she always envisioned her role of a spouse to be submissive, agreeable, and in this case, sexually available. With age, she had evolved in her discovery of Healthy ME. This also resulted in the changing some of her views about sex. After birthing four children and transitioning through menopause, her body was ready for a change and she was ready to speak out. For about a decade, she stayed silent about "faking the levels of pleasure" she experienced with her husband. In a desperate effort to continue a healthy sex life, they explored multiple sex toys, tactics for stimulation, and role play. These efforts just weren't enough. Weighing out the pros and cons of alternative methods, they decided to lay down some ground rules and came to the decision of trying to incorporate additional partners.

So there I was in my office, sipping on my coffee, trying to hold together some kind of poker face as my couple intake consisted of two hyperactive sexual people in their early 70's looking at me with the expectation of pulling a magical solution out my framed degree to help them achieve orgasms again. Yeah, I found myself pretty confused. Basically the shock of their open minds caught me off guard, and after my moment of stupidity, I became intrigued and joined in on their mission. It was really brave of them to come in because they felt so isolated in their desire to maintain a Healthy US in regards to sex. The basic conflict came from a lack of sexual communication and the misunderstanding of how to communicate pleasure to each other. It was beautiful in the perspective that they both still considered and saw each other as they did in their early 30's. It was also so difficult to bring up valid facts that their bodies and hormones were evolving and this meant focusing on not only sex, but change in the honesty of their sexual communication.

Sexual Conflict

Sexual conflict may resemble symptoms of regular conflict, but in cases such as a couple who holds back honesty to any degree, it can be more sensitive in nature, simply because of the vulnerability it entails. As couples go through transitions of having a new baby, death of a parent, changes at work, or physical and medical issues, sex is usually one of the first components to be neglected.

As couples work on the foundations of becoming a Healthy US, they can also slowly repair the sexual conflict that can often be a very silent but deadly factor in their relationship. Overcoming conflict depends on where it begins. Physical sexual conflict affects men and women differently. Men may view difficulty in arousal as a symbol of weakness or a representation of failed masculinity. Women may view "sex pain" as being incompetent overall and translate this into fear of being abandoned for failing as a loyal spouse. (view vs. own, sex pain)

Tactics and tricks for overcoming sexual conflict are available and address psychological, physical, emotional, and mental causes for conflict. In the focus of maintaining, repairing, or building a Healthy US, resolution starts with empathy and honesty. Hearing your partner's wants, wishes, desires, fears and concerns without becoming defensive or offering immediate solutions is invaluable. It shows respect and validates trust on an intimate level. Reflecting to each other that sex is not just intercourse, but so much more is the healthiest way to start the breakdown of sexual conflict and ultimately uphold the value you hold for one another.

A Healthy US takes constant attention and maintenance. Sex and Sexual Communication is a life-long process of exploration, vulnerability, and sincere commitment to self and US. Sex means intercourse, oral stimulation, mirroring each other's pleasure points by touch, and escaping the stigmas of society. It takes bravery to dismiss all insecurities and mindfully embrace the partner whom you've chosen to share this experience with. Sex is also the naked joys of laying on a couch or the fully-clothed, breath-taking longing for someone's voice and irresistible charm. As important as sex can be in a Healthy US, it's sisters Affection and Intimacy, have so much to do with how and when it is received and accepted.

Chapter 10: AFFECTION AND INTIMACY

Affection

In my clinical experience, it has been a trend for years that clients have a strong preference for scheduling on Wednesdays. What this has meant for me is scheduling back-to-back clients from 8 a.m. to 7:30 p.m., with no breaks. In better reference, it means maintaining empathy, wit, poise, strategy, and super human composure for 11 to 12 clients in one setting. As much as each of them mean to me, and as much as I sincerely care, I am delirious by the time I complete my session notes, consider looking at insurance claims, and lock the door.

In my own discovery of self, I have recognized some of the greatest impacts that simple affection can have on a human (or super human). Few people in the world actually comprehend a piece of what my day looks like on Wednesdays. Fewer have been brave enough to ask. Based on my disheveled appearance, I can empathize with people who don't know what I just put myself through and understand why they would just assume I am closed off and disconnected. This assumption of persona does not exactly lend itself to invitation of affection. Yet, at the end of a Wednesday, it's really the only thing I need just to pull myself out of the therapist role and back into a role of being just a person who had a long day at work. Well, that and maybe a martini.

On my most difficult days, my greatest gift is the hug from one of my most cherished friends. It's warm, embracing, empathic, and comes with no requests or expectations in return. It sometimes comes with a beer, which is pretty cool, but mostly, it validates me. It represents that someone does not consider me as cold or abrasive. They just see me as tired and with words. That hug tells me that I am going to be okay.

Psychological research has proven in so many studies the importance of affection and its connection to human survival. There's the famous study involving monkeys. A baby monkey is placed with a wire frame that has milk and a soft warm frame that does not. In the conclusion of the study, it was found that the monkey preferred to spend most of its time with the "warm frame" (This study actually explores nature and nurture but affection is part of it). Another study looked at birth rates and emotional development in orphans. Researchers compared healthy and unhealthy development in the long term with children who were cared for and given affection to babies who were difficult to nurture and ultimately received little handling. The babies who were picked up and given affection were significantly more adjusted. This trend can be examined for decades and longer; so it is important to justify that affection is not a trend, it is a necessity.

In the early stages of dating, mating, and forming human relationships, affection is given openly. This is a definite trend of newly romantic partners. A Healthy US is built on a sustainable foundation, so it is so disappointing and painful to see a couple withdraw affection toward each other out of fear, spite, anger, and emotional disconnect. In some cases it almost seems like affection can be used as a weapon or form of punishment and reward. If one partner gives in, they get reinforced with a hug. If that same partner reacts in anger, then they get put "in the box" or I guess in partnership language, the couch.

Affection holds a great depth in defining the culture of US and what is considered accept-able, normal, and significant. It is symbolic of the non-verbal communication of love and intimacy that exists in all forms of relationships. In session, it is very common for adults to break down when this topic is brought up. It brings out old feelings of neglect and interpretations of rejection and emotional confinement. It also symbolizes great strengths in couples who may not be extremely verbal but very much in sync with each other's needs and feelings.

"After months of reconciliation and efforts in repairing the damage caused by the betrayal of infidelity, we are very cautious about our verbal communication. We still had a lot of work to do in rebuilding our communication, but it was our affection that kept us focused on the end goals. As I would chop up vegetables and sauté chicken for dinner, he would just smile and grab my ass every chance he could find an excuse to pass me. I would pretend to get annoyed and swat him with the spoon, but really, I was flattered and sort of returning the affection with my response.

"Flirting in the kitchen would lead us to eating dinner together on the couch. We still didn't say much, but without discussion, we always made sure our knees were touching or that our toes met up on the ottoman. Affection helped us to regain trust even when we didn't trust ourselves to verbally always say the right thing. In our earlier years, we followed the rules of setting the dinner table and forcing discussion that was really meaningless small talk. And now, we not only show affection, but we always share a couch laying side by side. I never knew how intimate touching foreheads or laying a my head on his chest could be. I know it's not traditional communication, but our affection makes me feel alive inside, more than I ever did when we first met."

I can completely validate how much truth can come from non-verbal communication. I would even go so far as to say 80 percent of my analytical skills and therapeutic technique rely on observing body language, eye movement, and non-verbal social cues. So when I hear progress coming in the form of affection, I see it as being equally significant to any other form of connecting. Affection takes a great deal of insight for both individuals and the identity of the US unit. FOO plays a huge role in conditioning us for adult life and how we understand touch, communicate love, and receive non-verbal attention. In the case where one partner comes from a very non-affectionate family, openly exploring what role affection will play in the US unit created can create powerful positive change within that partner and possibly have a systemic effect on them.

Creating a Healthy US is all about having open discussions of boundaries and preferences. Some people just do not like to be touched. And after they go on to gain insight as a unit about fears and what touch and affection means to each of them, healthy negotiations for meeting needs and showing non-verbal love commitment, and intimacy can be established implemented.

If the reciprocation of affection does not go without saying, then looking further into the layer of intimacy and what expectations each partner brings into the unit of US can offer useful understanding of the direction US is going.

Intimacy

When I work with couples in high conflict, I always tell a story that revolves around the most unromantic version of intimacy. There are books with brilliant theories and terminologies on love and affection that describe how we give and receive, how we can learn more about truly embracing, and yet, I focus on where it could but does not get appreciated.

My greatest love story that I reflect on in my sessions goes something like this:

"I wake up to the horrible choice of alarm noise at an hour that is undeserving of my time. I make coffee, put my kids together for school in such a way that reflects I am a somewhat good mom who can braid hair and piece together a matching outfit. After gathering lunches, giving words of love and encouragement for my girls to get through their day of letter writing and toddler biting, I rush off in my 'hurry up and wait' 90 minutes of traffic, and begin my day of work. I have nine back-to-back therapy sessions, a 20-minute break to get from the office to the next job of teaching a 4-hour Psychology class, and then the journey home that will begin at 10:20 p.m. God willing there is not an accident and should only take about 30 minutes. On my journey home, I decompress slightly from my now 16-hour day rehearsing my thoughts of what needs to get done once

I get home. I know there are breakfast dishes, lunches to be made, coffee to preset for brew, some possible left overs that may not have mold but will suffice next to vending-machine options I had earlier, and I'm sure the dog was pissed off at me for something being gone so long, so I'll just anticipate that as well. Finally arriving home, I walk up to the door, begin to insert my key, and the smell of citrus soap is seeping from the door. I turn the key to the right, slowly open the door, and hear sounds of peace. Peace, not silence. There's casual music playing in the living room, a soft light coming from the kitchen, and the most beautiful sound I've ever heard. The dishwasher is running. My heart literally starts pounding, my eyes flood with tears, and my 10-pound work bag drops to my heels. Love. My partner thought of me. He knew my schedule that day. He did the daunting tasks that were mine. He showed me love by doing a service that I so desperately needed."

Yes, my greatest love story is that of how receiving love in my perception is to have someone help me in my time of exhaustion and make my life easier. My greatest love story is that I came home from a 16-hour day and had the responsibility of throwing on a tank top and shorts, and drinking the beer that had been poured as I changed.

This is an example I use when couples are

unsure of how to regain intimacy in their lives. It is not full of chocolates, flowers, cards, and gifts. It does not include physical touch or a candle-lit dinner. I never include the idea of compliments, or a celebration of money. There is no dancing, glass slippers, white horse, or heck, even handcuffs for those who are really excited to hear about the "it" love story. When I work on the components of love, I do not work on the ideals of love. In fact, I prefer to go more penguin style. "Here's your rock, are you down to accept it? Yes, cool, great, so lay the egg, I'll watch over it, go grab some food and I'll see ya in a bit when its hatched. Love. Teamwork. And go."

As couples begin their love story, they do not buy their first five minutes of impression based on romantic expectations and ideals of who is going to change the diapers and do the laundry. They quickly evaluate looks, determine if this person shows merit of learning their name, and then proceed on to introductions that usually include a name and a profession of some sort. The next five minutes are gained by a few quick nonchalant questions that subcategorize common interests, and if by the end of 10 minutes the spark overrides the rebuttals and unrecognizable red flags, the act of hormones and undeniable caveman instincts infuse our brains, therefore shutting down logic, reason, and ultimately all the crap that would have stopped us from engaging in the romanticism that sparks the opportunity of a new US.

Couples need to be reminded of this first interaction. I always ask, "Tell me about what it looked like when the two of you first started hanging out." My words are so intentional an yet confusing but well understood. I don't use the words "dating" or "love" or heaven forbid "having sex." I avoid labels because I don't want the current ideas of label that they may be using to interfere with the big picture. I want the story of their US. I want to know and uncover where their love started, what it looked like, how it evolved, and where they would like it to go.

You have control over questions and journeys that your brain has ingrained and perceived. You have control over where you, as a person, would like to see love be and look like in your life. In every first session, I give homework to couples that basically ask them this: Tell me what love could look like in your life; do not describe love with the past, present, or current partner unless it is the ideal. Tell me what you conceive love to look like.

Intimacy has a few different definitions for people. We know what we grew up seeing as far as how we received recognition, attention, and positive regard. We know what we saw our caretakers, parents, mentors do to model love. We developed our own ideas based on what we saw and either worked like hell to strive to be that great, or quite the opposite. Either way our goal was, is, and will perpetually and habitually be this: Avoid pain at all costs, and do what we think will work. But what we think will work is not always truth.

Couples often times have so much heavy conflict, and yet they want the same thing. They are saying the same thing, and just fail to show or articulate this in a way that can be understood. I am a person of concrete structure, so I typically draw pictures comprised of something slightly less artistic than stick figures. Bubbles, circles, lines, anything that demonstrates the picture I'm hearing in session but not obstructive to the view of what is really going on. Overall, I never draw out something I have not tried before, and I explain the love conflict through simple concrete logic that can be absolved.

Basically, Intimacy comes in 3 forms.

Romantic Passion

This is the hottest of the hot. Raging oxytocin flowing through the brain. Palms are sweaty, heart beats faster, pupils are slightly dilated, and oh the goose bumps (that seriously come from a text, a thought, and glance from this person). To be 13 has no comparison in how amazing this kind of intimacy appears to be.

I love my personality and it has a lot of quirks. So that fact that my friends are predominantly men mostly and forever is no shock to me. I relate cognitively over emotionally, I don't want to analyze off the clock, and I prefer sneakers to heels. There are moments however, when I must turn back into a caring emotional human and hear the unguarded stories of my man friends who have entered unsuspecting territory of post revolving door excitement. My man friends need to divulge the story based on feelings that all of us relate to, and all of us work so hard to regain of what is to be told.

One evening, as I sat in observation at a somewhat up scale little outside dive bar, I took in my atmosphere in observations of the human dating pool. Girls were doing their typical hair flips, men were scratching the back of their heads puzzled in coming up with the right phrases and words to lure in their prospects of beauty. The crowd of noise and ambiguity grew still and quiet and one of my buddies sat next to me starring at his half-sipped on vodka soda. Being the loyal and caring female to the man friends, I ask what is on his mind. After a pause, he stirs his drink, looks up at me and says that he's lost his girl. He tell me his tale, and this is where I define Romantic Love.

"My bros and I were ironing shirts, mentally prepping our charm and game, and ventured out to a party to celebrate New Year's Eve. I was going through a transition phase in my career and just started a new job, so I was focused more on hanging out with friends and just having a good time. As we walked in the door, girls with short dresses and cocktails in hand were crawling everywhere. I pretty much gave up this scene, but succumbed to the peer pressure of getting out and living life. I made my rounds saying 'Hi' to the people I knew; most of them were mutual friends, a couple of business networking acquaintances, and some new faces that did not strike me as extraordinary. I walked into the kitchen to make a drink, and that is when all the music went silent and everyone's face became an obsolete blur. I saw her.

"She was wearing a simple but flattering black dress. She was so different from everyone else at this party. She had a smile that brightened the room and her eyes danced with laughter and joy. I could tell she was a little older than me, but she was definitely the most beautiful woman I had ever seen. I can't pinpoint the perfume she wore, but her fragrance just tickled my nose with curiosity and delight.

I gathered the courage and pulled out my 'A' game of charm, salesman, and persuasion. She was so engaging and confident; it only made me want to work harder and keeping up with her intelligence and finesse. She was blunt, open minded, sharp with the sarcastic humor. Two hours of solidarity flew by and our conversation equivocated to two best friends from 10 years ago catching up on love, life, work, and family. We stepped outside for a smoke in the pouring rain, and as she scurried to pull back her hair, I had to go with the moment and embrace what was the best move of affection I had ever made. That was our first kiss. It was lustful, passionate, and felt natural. It was as though we had been kissing for years.

"As the night grew late, we talked about future ambitions, we danced, we sang, we debated; we were us. I always prided myself on giving up the lifestyle of one-night stands and meaningless sex because it just got old. I felt like this girl was what I wanted and waited for. Sigh. We went back to her place, and I felt like we were on our honeymoon celebrating what could be the greatest love story ever."

As I sat listening to my friend pour out this chick flick of a story, all I could do was continue to listen and simply wonder where this perfection of a girl ended up. How could something so perfect and new and beautiful not exist, considering he was here telling me about it rather than continuing to dance with her? And the therapist came out in me for just a moment, as I could not help but ask where the hell this beautiful, yummy smelling genius of a woman was now.

"Well, we dated for a few months, we loved

deeply for a few months, but then I just ... I don't know ... missed being single and hanging out with my bros. She was great, and in fact, I feel foolish now, because she may be the one that got away. She needed someone secure and motivated and committed, and I just wasn't there in my life yet. I didn't get it then, but I think I get that now."

Here lies the definition of Romantic Intimacy. Lots of oxytocin, newness, fun, passion, joy, and then if just at the right moment, when the chemical hormones wear off, the compassion and trust don't form into a foundation of beliefs, values, and futuristic hopes. The commitment to a partnership is missed. Romantic love has a very important role in Western society, however, it must grow, or it remains the love we will always chase.

Friendship

When I talk about intimacy in friendship, it's not literally the intimacy that two friends share between each other. I am referring to a relationship that started out as romantic intimacy and developed into a greater level of love and respect, that now no longer includes passion or sex and affection. It's actually opposite of romantic love and brings in a discontent level of sharing. Typically, when couples come into session trying to work through infidelity or high conflict, they have a love that still exists, but is categorized by this type. Somehow, the burden of careers, stress, children, and life has lead them up to this disconnect but the truth of dedication and commitment still exists.

They have found solace is routine and structure. Strengths include stability, financial planning, organization, and common respect. They both long for affection and loving attention, but many fears of disrupting comfort hold them back from exploring what once was. These couples don't come into session yelling or cursing out accusations. They appear as the perfect picture of white-picket fences and simulated "right" answers adorned with articulate jests. Both partners are seemingly comfortable in their roles and have a symbiotic definition of partnership and understanding.

As I go on to explore with my open-ended questions, the agony of silenced pains, desires, and truths poor out and the real truth behind this common type of love is expressed.

"So, tell me about your routine and what you envisioned your lives looking like." This is my common open-ended statement that usually leads to some honesty and a jumping off point for reality to better something, whatever that may be.

"Well," they say, "he typically likes to get up at 5:30 a.m. As he showers, I get up and make his breakfast, same as always - 2 eggs sunny side up, and a side of bacon. Sometimes I like to add green onion, but I try not to change it up too much. I always put out the paper and cream for coffee. I don't like his creamer, so I have to be sure that we have separate creamers out. Actually, I prefer the taste of house blend and he likes breakfast blend, so I started brewing our coffee in two separate coffee makers so that our tastes wouldn't collide."

At this point, after keen observation, sessions of experience, and a reputation of being, well, blunt, I go ahead and ask or state some bold but obvious statements and questions.

"Tell me when the two of you stopped sharing a bed. What has that been like? Friction is not spilling into the room because it already filled my bamboo cilantro scented ambiance 20 minutes ago."

With looks of shock, but not offense, they continue. They describe the birth of their first,a well-planned out child and then the shock and surprise of their second. As many couples experience, with a combination of fatigue, nursing, colic, work deadlines, and time, they just thought it to be a better idea to sleep in separate rooms. First he started working from the couch and falling asleep. She grew too tired to put the baby back in the crib and nursed from the bed while letting the first child sleep next to her so she didn't feel less loved or left out. Then he became tired of the couch and moved into the guest room. In the earlier years of raising toddlers, they would try scheduling sex dates when the children would nap or if the grandparents would offer to babysit, but eventually, that died down. Sleep aways turned into opportunities for them as a couple to catch up on work or sleep, and 10 years later there they were with a beautiful home, promising financial portfolio, and day dreams of retirement and possible reconnection at a far-off beach destination. But, of course, that will come after they pay off college, weddings, and establish financial securities for their potential grandchildren.

This is real. This is the 1970s show based on perfection that makes us have wet dreams about marriage and false hopes about life. It's a blunt haircut and two paycheck aways from a doll-sized dream house and an ice pick in the foot. Responsibility can meet the face of mind blowing sex, and excuses are all that hold this version of US back from living the real ideals of partnership. This kind of love holds its own in good values and lifestyle, but I will in all respect to those relating say, there is more. Let us explore our third option.

The all Consuming Intimacy

This type of intimacy is the most work and the most rewarding. It's the true definition of partnerships, human connection, trust, respect, and commitment.

On a brisk morning in Dallas, I sat on a porch admiring a duck pond sipping on cinnamon and nutmeg coffee. As I looked to the left of me, I began to admire the this very charming couple who appeared to be in the late 60's. I could see the passion they shared as he rubbed on her knee and she sitting no more than 3 inches a part, gazing attentively to his story. They both grinned, brightly showing off the evidence of years of laughter and smiles. At one point she said something so funny his shiny bald head turned bright red as tears streamed down his face as he shook with laughter. At this point I just couldn't sit back and gaze. I saw a dynamic that I've read about, researched, written about, but now it was live and right in front of me. I walked over, smiled politely, and warmly engaged with them about how much appreciation I had for their pleasant affection. They were kind enough to let me in to their space and share highlights of their 47 years of marriage.

Three children, seven grandchildren, military travels, higher education were just a few pieces they identified as the strength and power to their continued love story. They each had strong career identities, firm commitments to each other, emphasis on spirituality, and open communication about sex and affection. This couple openly appreciated that life was and always would be full of struggles, and they also understood that as a team they could get through anything. Lovingly they held hands and smiled with admiration as they continued their brilliant love story sharing with me the joy and promise that this kind of love can bring.

The All Consuming Intimacy is built on many facets from that make up a Healthy US, however, within each unique couple, one thing stands as a constant: Respect is valued over defense. The ability to communicate with grace and honesty is derived from a mutual respect and foundation based on assertiveness.

I once had a discussion with a relative of mine on the topic of assertiveness. In his view, it was an appropriate word to use in mixed company when talking about a bitch. Completely taken a back in surprise, I died laughing, and then abruptly, stopped, scowled, and grew offended. If this were true, then I had some serious social issues, because assertive is one of the top three words people had always used to describe ME! In reality, especially pertaining to relationships, assertiveness is simply a form of direct communication stating what you want and how your prefer it. No demands, no complaints, Just simple direct statements.

"It makes me feel safe when you double check that the doors are locked before we go to bed."

"Its important to me that we make time to share our days. It helps me feel like I'm a part of your life when we're working such busy schedules."

See, that's all there is to it. Assertiveness. Statements made directly, with the intent of respect.

Maintaining the All Consuming Intimacy does not carry a burden of problem solving or judgment of who is right and wrong. It's the art of practicing listening with only the intent of asking for clarification and permission to take turns speaking. Many times couples will tell me the frustrations of wanting to vent about their day and feeling interrupted or not heard when their partner jumps in with an immediate response of resolution. Sometimes, it is just more satisfying to share a story or express a feeling without any response at all.

The All Consuming Intimacy also derives from excellent sexual chemistry and validation. If partners are comfortable enough to share and express stories in daily conversations (communication), then they also have the power to have excellent sexual communication, and that is where amazing affection, sensations, and yes, orgasms are embraced. If enough trust is built within the foundation of a relationship, then enough trust is built into the act of physical touch and the possibility of many Naked Couch

Sundays in the future.

Affection and Intimacy: Working Together in Love

I remember my grandmother doing laundry and going about her morning routine of making beds and putting fresh towels in the bathroom. She always went about her day as she pleased, but not a second off beat. The moment her four-o'clock talk show was over, she switched on the evening news and started making dinner for my grandpa who entered the kitchen precisely a quarter after 5 p.m. As routine would have it, a bottle of beer would go into the freezer, a box of wheat thins was pulled out of the pantry, and dinner was served to him in his designated recliner just before 6. After dinner my grandma would put on her printed mu-mu, snuggle up to watch her favorite prime-time show, and he would kiss her forehead goodnight as he made his way to bed for the night.

This is not the most romantic example of love, but the nature of the system had a low conflict flow to it. Each partner had their designated roles for contributing to the household. There was a demonstrated affection for efforts, and the idea of safety was rarely compromised. Later as my grandmother grew progressively ill from her autoimmune disease, she was more dependent on my grandpa and roles of care and affection changed drastically. It took all the energy she had to put on her makeup and curl up her hair each morning, all leading up to a very winded afternoon. She still did what she could though to show her love, even if it meant maintaining her beauty for his return home.

This glimpse of my Family Of Origin paints a description of where I learned how to show and receive love. FOO plays a significant role in how we develop our belief system and values that we take into our US relationships. For most of us, we go one of two ways: Strive intensely to recreate what we loved about our Family Of Origin or work extremely hard to avoid repeating any behaviors we experienced. As I spent most of my childhood and adolescent years watching these patterns my grandparents played out, I soaked in an idea of stable partnership that was predictable, giving, not exciting, not lustful, but overall safe.

Love can be demonstrated and received in some pretty simplified ways: Doing for others (laundry), verbal (loving texts), concrete (tiny gifts or tangible tokens), non-verbal (shoulder rubs or forehead kisses), and mindful attention (present in the moment focused verbal and non verbal attention). As we develop our own acceptance and culture of how we receive and understand love from our FOO's, we also subconsciously define with quick judgment (schemas) with little thought of love. What we've used as data to build up our schemas for love is very unique and subjective. Without open communications, our goo- intended love can turn against us and or our partners. Recognizing love from a partner and receiving it in the manner it was meant to serve takes practice, a good FOO. Understanding, and patience.

Affection and Intimacy work together in creating healthy boundaries and common ground for unifying a Healthy US. Demonstration of non-verbal communicative love shows validation and sincerity of emotions and reciprocity of warmth and physical connection. It is a very powerful tool in creating healthy vulnerability and establishing a different form of trust within the US unit. As it adds to the balance of intimacy and initiates clarity within the scope of the partnership, deeper understanding of individual needs, ideals, wants, values, and commitment can continue to evolve and be expressed with comfort and security. These two components of a Healthy US are also a staple for exploring the more fun aspects of creating memories and sharing common interests. Together, they enable compromise and effortless enjoyment in the aspects of recreational activities and social participation.

Chapter 11: FINANCIAL COMMUNICATION

I understand that affection comes in many forms. Hugs and kisses are equal to coffee brewing in the morning. In my life, it took me decades to understand how my dad was not a robot. He never showed emotions. Empathy is out of his realm. All I knew is that he worked hard everyday and his job came first. I always wondered as a kid how he could love his work so much by spending so much time there and not love me. Living in separate cities, states, or at some points countries, visitations were short and sporadic. So during the 7 to 14 days a year that I did get to visit, I just could not understand why he chose to be at work instead of spending time with me.

After going through a huge life transition or three, we sat at dinner one night. Just the two of us. He started talking about his past jobs and money as usual, but then he paused like he forgot I was his daughter and just started talking to me like a person. In this moment, I understood him. I also learned a very valuable lesson in communicating finances in terms of relationships.

Money is dirty. It's never easy to talk about. It causes conflict in decision making, prioritizing wants and needs, and is just basically stressful. The more money you have, the more you spend. The less money you have, the less you can buy. Most people have debt regardless of their bank account figures. Most people hope to retire. Most people have dream cars, boats, houses, vacations, and possessions that money can buy. But I always point out a couple of obvious scenarios.

First, money is a humanly made up value put into a system that has flaws. Money can buy a sports car. The sports car, however, does not get up and make you soup when you have the flu. The sports car does not hold you when your mother dies. Money comes and goes. The love that is unconditional from real connections is permanent until death.

Second, money has a different meaning to all of us. Our FOO plays a huge role in how we see money and make decisions in how to take care of it or lose it. Some may argue that money can buy happiness and in reference to instant gratification, I can agree. True happiness comes from all the components of having a holistic identity, and leaving behind a trademark of some kind that makes us feel like we had purpose in this world when we leave it. Happiness is subjective, so if you think money does it for you, then keep on going. In creating a Healthy US, be sure that your partner shares these same qualities and values, or at least respects and appreciates you for having them.

Healthy US looks at money in many ways, and in focus of creating a working relationship, I focus on how each partner can openly convey their ideas about spending, saving, and investing on a level that can be negotiated and not argued about.

Several years ago I started working with a couple who came in for help in communication. After a couple of sessions, I could see that they wanted to continue but one partner started to withdraw and shut down when we would explore the challenges they were facing. Always remember, the bottom line with anyone is that they want to feel safe and they want to feel heard. Safety looks like many things depending on the individual and feeling heard is just a way of feeling acknowledged and understood.

In our third session, one partner started yelling about credit cards and money and how he is "fine with being here in therapy but it's just another dollar spent." This couple was not low on financial resources. They both had very high paying jobs, minimal credit card debt, and awesome financial portfolios. Having full disclosure, I sat there for a minute and knew that money was the topic of the fight, but not the actual issue. I asked the partner who was withdrawn to tell me a little bit about what money meant to him and where he first learned about its meaning.

He talked about his parents divorcing in his late childhood. His father was wealthy and left he and his mother. She had a difficult time keeping up with the rent payments and at times they had their utilities cut off. As a teenager he got a part-time job to help support he and his mother. Over time, he was able to save enough money to add to his academic scholarships and went on to earn his degrees nearly debt free. Money for him established safety and protection. He saw it as something to take care of because he knew how it felt to not have any and had the will to never feel that way again. As his partner sat next to him, tears just flowed out. His partner had never heard about this part in his life. All that had been expressed is the need to be controlling over the finances. No explanations about anger and credit card purchases and frustrations over going out to eat had ever been broken down into detail.

As I validated his vulnerability and observed the emotional turmoil I reflected; excessive spending jeopardizes your what you see as safety and your partner appears to be taking your safety away.

Money is one of those funny topics that all couples argue about at some point or another. About 90 percent of the time, money is just a topic that is an indirect frustration from the real issue. A Healthy US should discuss money with objection. Both partners should share the experiences from their FOO, current ideas about money and what it means to each of them, and finally, come up with a plan that each is comfortable living with. Seeking out expertise to further execute this plan is also a great way to bring in a mediator and redirect clarification if needed.

Sitting at the dinner table, looking at someone I know so well but see as such a stranger, I learned my financial lesson. He told me that the only way to show your family you love them is to make sure you can provide for them. It may mean that you live a part from them and sacrifice having marriages. No one else in this world is going to take responsibility for taking care of your family but you. You are all they have. It's your job to make money no matter what so that you know they are going to be okay until they can take care of themselves.

This philosophy may not be congruent to mine that facilitates a Healthy US or hell, even a Healthy ME. The lesson I learned though was that at least with this clarity, I could understand the reasons he chose work over me. It was out of love. It was not the kind of love I would prefer to receive, but at least I could understand that it was done out of love. In working with couples, this is the best place to start the financial talk. Address each partner's intentions because if nothing else, clarity can offer peace and that can evolve in to comprise and acceptance.

Chapter 12: CONFLICT AND RESOLUTION

Conflict

"Wow. You just don't give a fuck. If you were on a deserted island with one fuck to give, and I was there with you with a whole treasure chest of fucks to give, I wouldn't give you one. My fucks to give are valuable and I wouldn't use any of them on you. My fucks are just not meant to be given. They're just mine."

This is what I call the perpetual "Hallway Sex" moment, where the only sex going on at home is the yelling match of "F-You… well F-You too" while passing each other down the hallway. This is also a very common response to aggravated conflict. As I was talking about some brain storming ideas when writing this book, I brought up conflict with a friend and colleague of mine, and as he reflected on my ideas, this is the response he related to it. I appreciated the humor, as well as the literal translation of his response. I sit in my office daily hearing comments such as these, if not worse. The bottom line is not vulgarity; it's the simplicity of how much anger our partners can bring out in us! One of the more consistent patterns I see in couples with conflict is that the better they know each other and the more intimacy they share, the better they get at pushing buttons and bringing out the worst in each other's tempers if proper listening is not established.

In many scenarios, a response such as this comes from many unresolved conflicts that end in an outburst of hurtful words and flared tempers. Unfortunately, these conversations also include words that can't be taken back or forgotten, and diminish hard-earned trust and respect formerly established. Resolution may come, and feelings of remorse or guilt may follow, but significantly, these words are interpreted as some form of truth causing long term effects from the pain they trigger.

One early Saturday morning, two people sat in a condo, sipping on some coffee. The She partner suggested making cinnamon toast from last night's left over French bread. She puts together the ingredients for breakfast. Sounds of bacon sizzling in the pan, butter microwaving, and the lyrics to an Indie alternative song fill the void of silence drawn from conflict created during the night before. As the smells from baking bread seep from the oven and draw in warmth and comfort of cinnamon and sugar childhood memories, the She partner begins to reflect on happier times while attempting to show love slicing fresh strawberries hoping to make amends. As her partner sits on his phone sourcing through emails and work related leads, she begins to wonder how far her efforts will take her through this day. Will this breakfast of affection draw him nearer to her? Will he notice that she touched up her hair and make-up before leaving the bedroom to say good morning? Will he even see that she is trying to express remorse and achieve resolution with this selfless act? Fears of betrayal begin to cross her mind.

This breakfast represents an act of resolution and love. This breakfast is not just sustenance for a Saturday morning hunger. This cinnamon toast holds meaning far beyond the smaller scope of traditional roles and duties. It's a peace offering. It represents a talent that once won over his heart and impressed him with a potential of what his future life could look like. The perfection of gooey bread and crisp bacon represents her domestic talents that broke her a part from all other female companions. Her fear derives from the patterns of disappointment, rejection, and failure to meet expectations and forgiveness from her lover. Her thoughts expand into sadness and anger because as this breakfast reaches its peak to perfection, and the smells fill the room, her partner remains disengaged, disconnected, and in her eyes, unappreciative.

The fears have now escalated in to silent frustration and quickly turn into resentment. Internal comments like "I don't need this shit. He was the one who was wrong last night … I tried reaching out and cuddling in bed as he just turned over to snore … I could be having brunch with someone who really gets me and really cares about me … I hope he chokes on

his coffee…" As she starts to plate the breakfast items, her racing thought remains silent no
longer. Aggravation has reached its peak, and
now she speaks out loudly expressing words
that have been suppressed for quite some time.
"Here is your stupid breakfast! Thanks a lot for
doing nothing! I bet you won't even say thank
you! Make sure you use two forks so I can have
even more dishes to do once your done! You
don't care about anything but yourself you
selfish asshole!"

Now we have flying breakfast. Cinnamon
toast is now cinnamon glue stuck to the wall.
Bacon has officially become the literal description of "when pigs fly," and china, that took
hours to pick out at the wedding registry, is
now crumbles of sediment scattered across
the tile floor. The conflict from last night, that
we cannot even remember the beginning of,
has not gone away. It has erupted, and with it
carries the last 6 months, maybe even the last 6
years of withdrawn words, misinterpreted acts,
and countless hours of pity remarks whispered
under each other's breaths.

The She has had her fill of misinterpreted
perspective, lack of appreciation, and stakes
her claim to apologies, hypothetical rights to
the wrongs, and quick response to her actions.
However, the Nick in this conflict is not going
to bite. He does not remember an argument
from last night. He was tired, and full of pasta,

108

and passed out after crawling in to the warm comfort of his bed within seconds. He woke up this morning thinking about the deals he needs to close by end of day (he also does not see that Saturdays are for bonding, to him, they are another opportunity for accomplishment). So to his dismay, he has a woman who is unjustly screaming and throwing breakfast food all over the place. In his mind, he is just trying to figure out how this sweet woman who used to possess kind eyes and a bright smile turned so damn crazy over bacon and coffee.

This guy's guy is just waking up and going about his business as usual, and to the best of his knowledge, doing nothing wrong. As his innocent safety of morning coffee and news articles is being threatened, he loses tolerance for "crazy" and he is not considering a response full of apology or remorse. He has been cornered by a live angry She partner. There is only one response for this pattern of negativity in his mind. Set her straight. Tell her how this is going to end. Show his partner that her behavior is not only unwarranted, but how it will no longer be tolerated. Like a cornered animal, he now must fight back, defend his territory, and speak from raw emotions. Kindness and love are out. This is war, this is defense, this is survival.

The "Hallway Sex" response to conflict (and flying breakfast) is now interjected. This blunt and emotional language coming from the threatened guy's guy.

Yes, I told you that I am no stranger to the curse words, and this story is just one version of many told by the relationships that you and I find ourselves so puzzled in at times. They come from feeling vulnerable, trapped, stuck, isolated, lonely, and so very exhausted from small arguments we have chalked up to bull shit. We love our enemy so much! Why are they being so stubborn and difficult! And yet, after the storm of our argument has passed, we sit with guilt and resentment wondering where to go from here. How has our person we have so intricately developed our identities, livelihoods, and daily routines with become this magma of uncertainty and heartache? The one thing that binds the toxicity of what has become is the act of Will. Will is the foundation, the residue of previous passion, the hope of future in the pool of confusion and uncertainty. Will is the object left in our scope of US, and it's what opens our ears to hearing new perspectives and real solutions to what looks like stupid arguments that have built up into concrete conflicts.

As couples in high conflict enter my office, my first evaluations begin with their non-verbal cues. I observe their proximity to each other on the couch. Are their legs crossed with feet touching? Is one wrapped up within the safety of themselves while the other has an open arm extending over their partner's shoulder or knee? I watch to see if they make eye contact with me, the floor, or each other. Then I begin to ask just a few open-ended questions. "So tell me about yourselves, what brings you in today?" I set the mood to feel like three old friends getting together for coffee after a decade of life has happened to us. As they open up and regurgitate their first meeting, the quick and dirty version of where conflict began starts to unfold. I hear and see patterns that they have grown to normalize. The culture of their boundaries and barriers slowly unveil. This is when polite coffee mood transitions into heated multiple cocktails on an empty stomach territory. As I start to dissect the triggers that bring out the truth, I also start to identify the indivisible pains that have meshed into resentment and fear.

   "It's been 10 months since we last shared intimacy or a bed. My skin crawls every time he touches me while I'm cooking in the kitchen. The sound of his chewing is like nails on a chalkboard. I feel like every word that comes out of my mouth is going to be swallowed whole and spit back out at me with criticism and contempt as though I'm a bacteria that grows in the wart of a villain. I've tried to stay silent hoping the stress would just blow over. I've tried communicating but I typically get nowhere and I either start crying from frustration or shut down. Usually, he just gets irritated and walks away. The worst part about any of this is the devastation of feeling so lonely in a room where I'm not alone. I miss being loved, touched, valued as a person. I miss being appreciated and desired."

Oddly, much of our conflict begins with good intention and a display of love or affection that has been misinterpreted. From this, feelings of pain and rejection start to cultivate and our coping defenses ignite subconsciously leading to our primal or learned reactions in violation of safety. Depending on the level of interpreted offense, we either quietly file away this incident or react in preservation of self. Either way, the experience, if not dealt with, will become an impression that can be used as a survival resource later.

Resolution

"After dating for 6 months, we decided to move in together. It just made sense. Fewer expenses, no more living out of a back pack. We were in love and that is what we trusted to get us through anything. Of course we had our transitional adjustments and had to learn a system that allowed us to function in our daily activities, but it's hard to pinpoint how we got to this point.

"One day I got out of work early and decided to make a specialty cake we had drooled over on a cooking show we recently watched. After traveling to two grocery stores and one chocolate boutique to gather the ingredients, I finally made it home. Well! They don't call it specialty without reason and that cooking show did not do justice to the actual labor. Three hours later, I have this cake. I put out pretty plates, set up some music, and freshened up a bit. As my partner came in, I was grinning ear-to-ear bursting with excitement about this accomplishment I made for him. He made a casual compliment, like "oh that's nice," grabbed his piece, and changed the music to some celebrity entertainment show."

When I sat with this couple, they were coasts a part on the couch, arms folded, and completely withdrawn from each other. This story about cake symbolized the core of criticism, resentment, guilt, and pain. After further exploring the meaning behind cooking for his partner, the unspoken FOO culture, and other acts that have gone unappreciated, the partners were able to see how simple misinterpreted love had now escalated in to mistrust and contempt.

Showing love takes a certain level of vulnerability and finesse. As we start out developing our US culture, there is a lot of given trust and mutual respect, partly because it's new and untainted.

In addressing conflict, resolution comes from a deeper source, the trigger that instigated conflict. Conflict resolution starts by identifying the learned patterns of defense and prolonged validation the couples have cultivated over time. Each partnership develops basic foundations to their Healthy US, and sometimes when trust is violated or rejection is interpreted, old habits of defense become second nature and the established healthy patterns of resolving conflict are disregarded. The are of conflict resolution comes from that primitive early stage of the US unit. The careful use of words, polite gestures, raw exposure of charm and acceptance. The tools for resolving conflict have always been present, they've just fallen underneath a mask of repeated patterns of miscommunication.

The bottom line to conflict resolution is simple. Trust that your partner wants to stop arguing and is just as ready as you are to put this puzzle back together. Allow for clarification and do not expect an apology. Validate where there are differences and assert your feelings with ownership rather than blame ("I felt … when," rather than, "you made me feel when you"). Assess the severity or repetition of the conflict and decide if there is a bigger issue to resolve or if there is a simple solution available if necessary. Assume that pride has no place in conflict resolution. Only clarity and acceptance. Lastly, move forward with respect and forget about holding a grudge. Conflict resolution can be practical and is one of the few areas where logic is really better than addressing emotions saturated in anger and stubborn entitlement to being right. Conquering conflict is such a useful pattern in a Healthy US, especially when US has gone under the stress and strain of multiple responsibilities.

Chapter 13: PARENTING

Parenting

Hand-crafted embroidered nylon seemingly water resistant reflects bright in the sun. The detailed embellishments of tribal art work sewn in bright yellow stands out strong against the diamond patterned gray and white hues of the fabric. In one side pocket, a carefully measured bottle of liquid stays cool keeping qualities of its one-part clear, two-parts Caramel color. In the other side pocket, a plastic credit card holder that once meant freedom and debauchery in a city full of lust and strippers; dangling beside it, the keys that once opened something sexy, fast, and only had room for two. In this pocket, truth is disguised.

The bottle: It's a sippy cup. Two-parts Apple juice, one-part water so we don't over serve sugar. The card holder doesn't remember strippers, unless fully-clothed girls who resemble animal creatures singing about sharing and the alphabet count. Oh the keys! Yeah, its still fast, but modified with DVD screens, a car seat, and the latest technology in window tinting.

The man that proudly wears this cross-body, back-pack thing in marketed "man colors" does not just wear a diaper bag. He wears it as a badge of honor. It's the symbol of "Yeah! That's right! I got laid, I got a bag, and I got a little replica of me! Beat that sucka!"

Watching the men at bars with playgrounds is quite possibly one of my favorite past times.

I can see the validation of getting away with being a 5-year-old while having the adult privilege of drinking a beer and maybe touching mummy's boobies later if "I can keep this kid entertained long enough." I enjoy watching parents interact because it's a moment when the US puts everything else aside for the joy of the little thing(s) they have created.

In some partnerships, the decision of having children is part of solidifying a version of a Healthy US. Couples share visions of future little league games and ballet recitals. They negotiate their ideals of parenting and buy professional books on organic baby foods and collect brochures for the best preschools. Once this beautiful little person is born, the tears of joy from all that has been planned and hoped for celebrate this life changing miracle of US and the beauty that US can create.

The rights of passage into parenthood can mean something different within each individual of US. In my rights of passage, I recall the first social media quote I used to ambiguously announce my pregnancy, "Goodbye Happy Hour, Hello Baby Gap!" It was my first attempt in embracing how my life would change. I could only imagine that my stomach would never look the same, my "Sunday Funday" friends would go on with out me, or that my date nights would be scheduled around play dates.

Prior to being the father he is today, I enjoyed seeing the transformation of one of my first colleagues I met after completing my licensure hours. My girls were 1 and 2 at the time and I worked a full-time administrative job while starting up my private practice in the evenings. Needless to say, I was busy, tired, determined, and completely forgot what free time for myself looked like. There he was, just a cool single dude. He was well in to his career, always talking about cool concerts he went to, and could tell me about every local happy hour special based on the day and time.

A few short years later, I grew in my profession and learned to make time for myself. And there he was - both of us at the same concert venue, only he was working and loving life. This time, something was different. He was not bragging about cool happy hour spots and "dude stuff." He was bragging about a baby that was coming in just a few short weeks, and it was his! There was no way for me to summarize, interpret, quote, or capture the the experience of his passage into parenthood the way he could. This is my favorite narrative of what transformation into Healthy ME, Healthy US and Healthy DAD can look like.

Being "admitted" to fatherhood
By Matthew Girard

If you have ever found yourself at almost any kind of event, you've most likely been asked to present either your right or left hand and then have had the door person strap a band around your wrist to signify your admittance.

Being a journalist, a sports fan and an avid live music lover, I have worn many a wristband throughout the years.

Some wristbands I've worn for days and others were discarded at the end of the night.

Many of those events have been memorable experiences and I've even saved a few of the wristbands as keepsakes to say "I was there."

With the wristbands that have made my collection, I often find myself reminiscing about the memories made and the experiences I've been through while wearing those wristbands.

Last Saturday morning, I held out my right hand to have a band strapped around my wrist so that I could be "admitted" to the most memorable and rewarding event of my life.

This wristband didn't contain any cool technology to track your experiences at a festival or was emblazoned with a beer company sponsorship. This wristband was a simple piece of paper laminated on to a pink background and wasn't given to me by some big, burly door man, but it was clear that this wristband would become a part of my collection.

Just after 2 a.m., a nurse admitted me to fatherhood after the birth of my daughter.

For the next two days, I wore that obnoxiously pink wristband proudly as I learned the ropes of being a father for the first time.

After bringing my new family home on Monday and finally getting the chance to relax, I looked at my wrist and realized that much to my surprise, the wristband had survived the previous 48 hours, despite its simplistic design.

With a quick snip of the scissors the pink band slid off of my wrist, but I knew this wasn't just any wristband that would be discarded in the trash.

After changing numerous diapers, soothing a fussy baby with many laps around the room and sleeping on an incredibly uncomfortable couch, the wristband was there the entire time "recording" every joyful memory of the beginning of my daughter's life.

It wasn't long before the pink band joined my collection of cherished tokens.

There will surely be more bands that will be wrapped around my wrists to signify my admittance to various events in the years to come, but none will ever be more special to me than the plain, pink band that admitted me to the most amazing event of my life.

Events such as these are built on emotions, individual transformations, and significant elements that challenge and broaden the scope of a Healthy US. As individuals, we need to share our personal feelings during this transition. It helps build the bond between new parents to offer support during time of exposed weakness, fatigue, and joy.

Parenting is a significant component in a Healthy ME for many people. In the exploration of a Healthy US, I focus on the act of parenting as a frontal unit built with strength and collaboration. Through the primary years of development, additional children may be added, tribulations of financial discord, cognizant planning for sex, and cultural shift in support systems all become a new type of "norm." Children are a humbling element to a Healthy ME and a Healthy US. They keep us grounded when all other parts of life can seem so unpredictable.

Children are also a trauma. They add an element of compromise and shift in routine. They demand energy that sometimes doesn't exist. At the end of the day, as they snore peacefully with a lovey in one hand and innocence in the other, the partnership responsible for making them, is awaiting for attention as well. In relationships, we sometimes forget to switch roles from parents to partners and as conflict or stress goes unresolved, children can become the scapegoat in avoiding the real issues. Parents may dilute bigger issues into petty arguments around sharing bath time or homework help. Love is spread thin and affection is reserved for lunches and middle school locker drama. College tuition replaces vacations and second honeymoons. After sending off your mini-me's out into the world, you sit in this empty nest that was once purchased as a symbol of your love and commitment to each other.

Maintaining a Healthy US while balancing a healthy parenting unit takes dedication and values its first intent: Friendship. Despite arguments and life adversities, we stick together. The conflicts our children go through in every stage of development remain their conflicts and our role is to see them through it with guidance, love, and support. It is not our role to side against each other and create a division. It is not our opportunity to win a race and see who can outshine who by undermining and manipulating favoritism. A Healthy US always unites and openly shares fears, concerns, joys, and celebrations of triumph.

Co-parenting

In situations where couples decide that
romantic partnership is not the best fit for the
family, the next best practice is exploring how
each can be a Healthy ME and work together to
be a Healthy Parenting US dynamic. Children
have nothing to do with the unresolved issues
that occur with adult conflict and mistakes.
They give partners, who just don't work out
romantically, an opportunity to grow in the best
possible ways toward communication, coopera-
tion, and expression of how much they have in
common when it comes down to loving these
special people they've made together.

"It was my first daughter's preschool graduation. She wore a little blue cap and gown with a
tiny gold tassel. As she walked in the line with
the other 5-year-old's, they played the traditional graduation march song. She starts looking
for us as she finds her place in the assembly;
then as she makes eye contact, she throws up
two hands waving and smiling so proud with
excitement. In this moment, all that mattered in
the world was that smile, those big brown eyes,
and that goofy little giggle. Together, we made
that. Together, we accomplished keeping her
alive, healthy, and evidently happily adjusted.
We may not be the traditional view of parenting, but there we were, sitting side-by-side in

the front-row folding chairs, crying like babies as our little angel took her first step toward a new transition."

The relationship of co-parenting has its own unique grace in compromise, respect, and trust. In moments of frustration during partnership, the idea of crying or showing emotions is just a form of weakness because we're too busy with our power struggle. In Healthy Coparenting US, there is no power struggle. It's completely liberating and safe to be exposed and share emotional moments that are directly related to our children.

Parenting, in general, should always have one intention: To do what is in the best interest of the child. There will always be variables from culture to environment, limitations and expectations. Even as a Healthy Me or Healthy US, we're human, so it's not always going to be the ideal we plan or as perfect as we'd like it to be. As long as it comes from love and good intentions, the kids are going to be okay, and the adults are going to get through it, one way or another. Just remember, in all the scenarios, we have to work together.

Chapter 14: OVERCOMING BETRAYAL

Betrayal Defined

"My girlfriend is such as ungrateful bitch! She doesn't appreciate anything I do for her. She wouldn't know what love was even if Cupid smacked her upside the head with his bow and arrow!"

This is how I started my morning one delightful Monday. It was a second session with a couple who described being in deep conflict and wanted help with communication. They were so angry that one partner sat on the far end of the couch fixated on the tree outside the window and the other grabbed a chair from the waiting room and as close to the door as possible. The coffee table in between them was a literal island of separation that exposed just how distant they felt from each other. Calmly embracing this opening to our session, I asked about the context from which this accusation was drawn from.

"Well, here's just one example of how much I keep trying and she just keeps acting crazy! I wanted to do something nice for her when she got home from work. The day before she was griping about being overwhelmed with all the laundry and something about mountains in the bathroom I never see. I didn't really say anything and I sure as hell didn't want to stop what

I was doing in the garage, so she got all pouty like usual and stomped off to bed.

"The next day I got off work early and felt kind of bad for not paying attention to her, so when I got home I finished all the laundry. I washed it, dried it, even put it all away, which was a major task. It's a big deal to hang dress shirts and skirts and stuff like that. Well, when she finally came home from work, I stayed quiet in the living room hoping she would get all excited when she saw that the laundry was done and the closet and bathroom looked really clean and organized. Instead, she just put on pajamas came downstairs, made a sandwich and started watching TV. I was so mad. I did all that nice stuff to make her happy and it was for nothing! In fact, I went to the bedroom to set some mood lighting and she just left her work clothes in a pile on the floor! Like she didn't even get that I spent all of that time making it look nice and just went and messed it up again. Do you see now why she is so selfish!"

During this little episodic story of drama, I also watched the non-verbal reactions coming from her girlfriend. I could see where her face became defensive during parts of the story, how her breathing changed during the climax, and how she completely shut down as the conclusion to this story was told. It's interesting in sessions like these because the couple is in a state of being in a stand off. They come in with one partner escalated in this power struggle with the other partner in a completely zoned-out, shut-down mode. The one thing they did agree on at this point was that they hoped like hell I was going to tell one of them they are right and the other they are totally in the wrong.

In response, I addressed the effort of doing laundry and validated the good intent. I acknowledged the suspicion and exhaustion of her girlfriend too. Then I took a leap of faith (and big picture perspective) and reflected on what I was really hearing. The anger and resentment from this client was a result of feeling betrayed. She was attempting to show love by doing all the laundry and when it went unappreciated, she took this as rejection of her love. Her feelings of disappointment and pain escalated into resentment of not being valued or good enough. This where the breakdown of communication builds into contempt and this form of betrayal can be the most toxic and difficult to work through. Another form of betrayal happened at the beginning of the story too. The girl friend who stomped off to bed also experienced rejection. Her rejection stemmed from an emotional disconnect when her partner was disinterested in what would make her happy and prioritized the garage work over her need for feeling loved.

It may all sound thrown out of proportion, and usually with silly examples of laundry or dishes, it is. I use the laundry example a lot when discussing betrayal because most people can relate to its meaning in some form and see how the actual betrayal is avoided (the big picture) and the hurt seeps out into multiple petty arguments like dinner, dishes, or locking the door. My focus is never in the details of the right and wrong, examples of bickering, or tiny injustices. It's always in the pattern of how each partner internalizes the pain and where the real pain actually started.

Looking into family dynamics and partnerships who share parenting, I see betrayal in the form of division of the US unit as a front when leading the family. As parents, a Healthy US may turn against each other in response to stress or problematic behaviors from the children. It's a form of betrayal when one partner feels undermined when choosing a form of discipline or setting a boundary. Betrayal can also occur when one parent seems too controlling or overbearing and the other parent feels the need to take on a role as the protector, siding against the US unit and joining the sibling unit. Ultimately, even when seeing how different forms of betrayal may appear in parental roles, it usually stems from a bigger picture issue and trickles down into the family system.

Betrayal may start out as dismissed frustrations and overlooked miscommunications of love, affection, and good intentions. But the problem with betrayal is how quickly it can snowball and how much power it can gain in such a short amount of time. After enough petty fights and rejections of attempts to show love, partners start holding on to grudges, turn to self preservation, and in some cases, look to fill the emotional or physical void that the US unit is not providing.

Infidelity

Infidelity is a primary specialty within my practice. There are hundreds of infidelity stories I could use as narratives to describe this form of betrayal, but the word pretty much speaks for itself. Infidelity is an act of going outside the US unit in pursuit of filling a void and alleviating unmet needs. In all cases of infidelity, results include hurt and pain, defiance of trust, opportunity for silenced truths. Infidelity is not about blame. It's a symptom of what is being neglected in the relationship.

After a series of failed communications, unresolved conflicts, insecurities within individual partners, enmeshed patterns from FOO, and other life distractions, couples eventually lose sight of what a Healthy US ever was, and lose control over the US dynamic. When I address the basic premise of the betrayal, I make an assessment for where the couple currently stands in intentions for growth and start the process for ideas in moving forward. Identifying the patterns that lead up to infidelity can lead to amazing opportunities for growth, establishment of an even strong foundation, and development of empowering strengths for a Healthy US. This is very different from an approach of denial and blame (like jumping to the conclusion where both partners are to blame) because this approach reinforces failure, guilt, and gives the betrayal its own identity as though it's the third partner in this "broken" US dynamic.

Working Through Betrayal

Betrayal is very painful and breaks down important healthy components such as trust and respect. Working through betrayal is a very brave and resilient commitment and this decision alone marks the first step in rebuilding a Healthy US.

Examining FOO, the happy beginnings of the relationship, and revisiting times of strength and joy is the next step. We need to remind ourselves of that first kiss and initial charm we fell in love with because in this complicated mess of hurt, there are still beautiful moments that were built before now. Progress takes time, and resistance toward trusting each other is to be expected.

The journey of working through infidelity is to be clear of the first rule of thumb in a Healthy US: We show up each day by choice, not obligation. We appreciate being chosen, and reciprocate this appreciation every day we show up. Small steps toward progress need to be celebrated and respect of space, time, and support need to be offered during the more difficult days. Betrayal does not have to be a permanent way out, but without a daily check in on where the intimacy goals are going, it might lead to a mutual understanding that this symptom is part of a trauma that may not be healed.

Divorce and Separation

"Honey, life happens as you plan it." This may be the best statement of wisdom my mother ever offered to me. She's always had a tendency to hold back her opinions and keep words of advice to a minimum. I always wished she had been more outspoken about her thoughts and shared what I considered to be wisdom during different transitions I went through in life. Her style is more discrete and perhaps is her way of showing unconditional love without judgment. So when she spoke up and made this one direct statement, I listened and exhausted it as my daily mantra for several years to come.

Privacy, pride, and fear of disappointment describe the tip of the iceberg that my anxieties were based on. I was scarred of what people would think and how they would judge me. I never disclosed information about our marital conflicts or unspoken versions of betrayal and emotional disconnect. I had no clue about how this transition would impact my career or my reputation long term. I despised the fact that I would be another statistic in history as a partner who gave up. After all my perseverance in building up my strengths and overcoming filial and economic adversities, I stood inches away from the line that would crush my efforts, expose my weaknesses, and go down on public record that I was an epic failure.

I never predicted that I would be my own specialty. After learning about all the struggles of single parenting, financial burdens, and the impact of how divorce spreads its pain systemically, I could not believe that I was still looking at this option as my final solution. Divorce was no stranger in the world that I came from. My parents, grandparents, uncles, and distant extended family had all gone through divorce, for some, multiple times. I knew this transition would be unpredictable and devastating, but all I could see in front of me was this dark tunnel of loveless entrapment and would never see a light at the end.

Divorce holds a place in the exploration of a Healthy US because it factually is an option and for some partnerships, is the last solution to gaining clarity and solidarity. Divorce offers closure and enables exponential growth opportunity if insight and deep amounts of process are included. Although it sounds contradictory, some partnerships need to dissolve so that each individual can embrace exploration in becoming a Healthy ME, which makes two Healthy ME's, and at some point, grow into a newer, better version of a Healthy US, even though the US dynamic may change.

As couples explore divorce, they often experience bi-polar extremities of emotions. It's common to question this decision during and after the transition. As each partner goes through the mental and emotional process, a variety of strengths and new challenges are gained. It's a process of grief and loss, multiple variations of anger, helpless limbo and uncertainty, and takes up a great amount of energy. The one obvious answer is that at some point, there is an end to the transition.

Some couples choose other options for working through betrayal and moving forward, such as separation. I've worked with couples who remain legally married for particular circumstances and agree to have open relationships with other people. Some separations include living in different households or states while continuing to share financial responsibilities. Separations have been known to allow for time and space that can lead to stronger friendships and partnerships between individuals. Healthier versions of people can blossom and reconcile or gain more certainty about choosing dissolution in the US unit. Most importantly, this is a transition of proactive growth and clarity. It should not be used as a state of limbo. Should open communication and clarification be dismissed, greater levels of pain and stress can accumulate and lead to more difficult forms of closure.

Betrayal, as we have explored, can appear in many forms and be interpreted and perceived in many versions. Betrayal does not define whether or not the US unit is healthy or viable. It plays a role in the decision-making model of how a Healthy US is going to evolve, grow, and thrive or how a Healthy US is going to move forward in separate directions. It does not dilute into weakness and failure. It does not curse us to live a life in solitude or necessarily predict failure in future relationships. As we grow and learn from experiences involving pain from betrayal, we become stronger and more certain of who we are and what healthier versions of ourselves can look like.

Chapter 15: SUMMARY OF HEALTHY ME, HEALTHY US

Finding what feels truly healthy to you is a process. It takes time and evolves with the directions life takes you in. Stability and safety come from insight and perception. Love and intimacy grow in capacities we allow. I don't believe things get better. That idea leaves too much out of my ability to find control within choice. I believe our perception can change and we can feel differently about anything. We can see better in ourselves, our situations, our relationships, and our partners. We make the choice to find better and execute our vision to see it through.

Becoming a Healthy ME offers growth and change. This process offers clarity to own who we are and appreciate all we do even if no one else in the world can validate us. We own up to our talents and our strengths. We exude confidence and take advantage of free will over pre-conceived destiny. And most of all, we have so much to offer and see clearly who deserves our investments of ourselves.

A Healthy US can happen at any stage in life. It can evolve from years of tumultuous failures or be established within the first meeting. The idea of what healthy looks like in a partnership is unique to each relationship that is formed. If it feels right and it functions for you, then you know it is a good system for you. We are fortunate to find people we connect too, even if it doesn't last a lifetime. These connections make us wise, and help us to develop insight of who we are beyond our comprehension had we never gone though these experiences at all. Power lies in the bounds of passion. When we embrace it, we can do anything.

Exploring the Whole Self

Different Pieces of Identity:

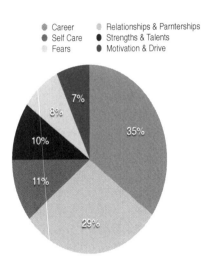

- Career
- Self Care
- Fears
- Relationships & Parnterships
- Strengths & Talents
- Motivation & Drive

Career:
What does Career Mean to Me? (EX: Leadership, Provider, Game Changer)

_____
_____
_____

What am I passionate about? What Motivates ME?

_____
_____
_____

What would I consider my Purpose in this life? What Meaning does it have?

_____
_____
_____

Strengths and Talents:

Relationships and Partnerships:

Family of Origin (FOO):

Supportive in My Life:

Stressfull:

Positive Energy (gives energy):

Negative Energy (takes my energy):

Self Care:
Physical:

Mental:

Emotional:

Professional Counseling, Supervision, and Public Speaking
Savannah Tucker, LPC_S
4425 Mopac South Bldg 3 Suite 505 Austin TX 78735
512-709-6475
www.centexlpcs.com

Made in the USA
Columbia, SC
30 May 2019